'Almost 6000 people die by suicide each year in the UK, leaving almost 6000 devastated families. Sue Henderson's personal story captures the distress, the disbelief, the questioning – but also the need to recover, to survive as a family. She brings a professional eye and even a wry humour to this most painful of subjects. It's an unusual book about a frequently hidden topic.'
– Prof Louis Appleby, Chair, National Suicide Prevention Strategy Advisory Group

'My personal experience and my work as a funeral celebrant has made me acutely aware of the loneliness and desperation that bereavement, and particularly bereavement through suicide, can bring. This book is not another self-help manual…it's a warm embrace from a kind friend: you will feel its arms come around you offering comfort, support and, above all, understanding.'
– Kate Buchanan, Humanist Celebrant, Humanist Society Scotland

'This is an honest and moving account of Sue Henderson's life following her husband's suicide, detailing the highs and lows of bringing up two small children alone while trying to come to terms with such devastating loss. Her resilience and incredible positivity shine through the pages, and her frank account of the emotional fallout is balanced with some sound theoretical information. A must-read for anyone affected by suicide.'
– Dr Mary Turner, Reader in Health Services Research, University of Huddersfield

'Reading Sue's book sent me on an emotional rollercoaster, which I didn't want to get off. I laughed at points, I cried at others, and at times I was so captivated I felt like I was experiencing their journey with them. Not only is this beautifully written book sensitive, honest and insightful about the life of a bereaved parent and the challenges this brings but it is relatable to all types of bereavement. I'm sure that others reading this will find reassurance and comfort as well as guidance and affirmation in relation to their own experience of grief.'
— Donna Hastings, Bereavement Co-ordinator, Richmond's Hope

'Sue's book gives a genuine, heart-warming and wrenching account of how suicide changes family life forever. With two young children, ever growing and changing in their understanding of their grief, Sue eloquently describes how she (and others) supported them in the days, months and years following Jon's death. Winston's Wish is proud to have been part of their story, which illustrates that the direction of grief is never straightforward but families can find their own "new normal".'
— Suzannah Phillips, Winston's Wish, the charity for bereaved children

THINGS JON DIDN'T
KNOW ABOUT

of related interest

I'll Write Your Name on Every Beach
A Mother's Quest for Comfort, Courage
and Clarity After Suicide Loss
Susan Auerbach
ISBN 978 1 78592 758 4
eISBN 978 1 78450 615 5

Rafi's Red Racing Car
Explaining Suicide and Grief to Young Children
Louise Moir
ISBN 978 1 78592 200 8
eISBN 978 1 78450 476 2

Luna's Red Hat
An Illustrated Storybook to Help Children
Cope with Loss and Suicide
Emmi Smid
ISBN 978 1 84905 629 8
eISBN 978 1 78450 111 2

Still Here with Me
Teenagers and Children on Losing a Parent
Edited by Suzanne Sjöqvist
ISBN 978 1 84310 501 5
eISBN 978 1 84642 580 6

THINGS JON DIDN'T KNOW ABOUT

Our Life *After* My Husband's Suicide

Sue Henderson

Jessica Kingsley *Publishers*
London and Philadelphia

The advice and information sheets from Winston's Wish in the 'Useful Resources' section are reprinted with kind permission from Winston's Wish.

First published in 2018
by Jessica Kingsley Publishers
73 Collier Street
London N1 9BE, UK
and
400 Market Street, Suite 400
Philadelphia, PA 19106, USA

www.jkp.com

Copyright © Sue Henderson 2018

Library of Congress Cataloging in Publication Data
A CIP catalog record for this book is available from the Library of Congress

British Library Cataloguing in Publication Data
A CIP catalogue record for this book is available from the British Library

ISBN 978 1 78592 400 2
eISBN 978 1 78450 766 4

Printed and bound in the United States

For Eilidh and Cameron, who make it all worthwhile.
In brilliant, technicolour memory of Jon

CONTENTS

ACKNOWLEDGEMENTS

This book is about Jon's, Eilidh's, Cameron's and my story, but neither book nor story would have been possible without the following people, to whom we send our thanks:

To Elen, Sean, Vicki, Sarah and their teams at JKP, for helping me to navigate the previously uncharted waters of the publishing world.

To Alan M, for your editorial wisdom, especially with regard to the semi-colons.

To James, for encouraging me that there was a different book to write.

To Cat, for the hill walks last summer which got me back to writing.

To Kate, Alan and Christine – my first readers and constructive critics, who told me this story was worth putting out in the real world.

To Carol-Ann, Eileen and Zoe, our child-care fairy godmothers in the early years.

To the staff at Winston's Wish, for their kindness and support. And to Donna, Ash, Kelly and everyone else at Richmond's Hope, whose calm wisdom and optimism have been invaluable.

To Louis Appleby, whose insightful words at a time of loss and chaos helped greatly, and stayed with me.

To all our friends and wider family we send huge thanks. To all of you who knew and loved Jon, and have helped Eilidh and Cameron to know him through your memories as well as mine. And also to our more recent friends who didn't know him but have been no less part of our lives and safety net over the years. Particular thanks go to all the surrogate dads, for being the next best thing; and to my top girls. You all know who you are.

And finally, our biggest thanks to our close family. To Jon's mum and dad, for showing their love for Eilidh and Cameron, even in the face of their own terrible loss. And to Mum, Dad and Julia: For picking up the pieces in the early years, and your constant love and care – we wouldn't be in such great shape now without you.

AUGUST 15TH 2001

Jon, my husband, took his own life at the age of 35. He left for work at 7.30, as usual. He kissed me, and our two children, as usual. He told me he loved me, which was not usual, but that didn't occur to me until later.

At 10.30, two police officers came to the door. I was changing our baby son's nappy – he was 19 days old. Our daughter, who was 27 months old, was with our childminder. I left the baby on the changing table to get the door. My first thought was that the police were there in connection with the speeding ticket Jon had picked up three days previously.

But I knew from their faces, and the fact there were two of them, and that they would have known my husband would be at work, and the creeping dread that filled me as I realised all of this in an instant, that this wasn't what they were there for.

I went back to fetch the baby. The very kind, very gentle police officers told me there had been an accident. My husband had fallen from Arthur's Seat in Edinburgh at ten past eight that morning. It looked as if he'd been out for a hill walk. But I knew it wasn't an accident. And so did they.

They stayed with me while I phoned my team mates at work. Two of them came immediately. I phoned my Dad at work in Manchester. He arrived that afternoon. The police managed to contact my Mum and sister who were both driving down the M6: Mum had only left us that morning after visiting to help us with the new baby. They both came back. I can't imagine how they managed to make that journey knowing what had happened.

I remember everything about that day in sharp focused detail. A lot of what has happened in the years since is vaguer, but that day and the ones leading up to the funeral are the clearest memories I have.

On that day I remember: my Dad in tears – I'd only seen that once before. Dad making all the terrible phone calls to tell friends and relatives what had happened.

Collecting our daughter and seeing the look on our childminder's face – Dad had phoned her to tell her the news.

Telling my daughter, in words she would understand, that her daddy had died and wouldn't be able to come home and be with us any more.

I remember having to face my parents-in-law, and the house filling up with friends who had heard the news and wanted to just be with us.

My breast milk dried up instantly as a result of the shock. We ate ready-cooked roast chicken from Tesco. I wondered if we would have to leave our home, and how I would support the children by myself.

And I remember knowing, absolutely knowing, that our lives had been instantly changed forever.

There was such clarity on that day, a clarity which I have rarely been able to summon in the intervening years. It felt as if I knew things and understood things immediately, and clearly. That was my experience of shock. Not something that rendered me distanced or cut off, but more connected and sure of things than I could have imagined. That certainty and clarity didn't last. But those earliest days are still etched in my mind.

* * * * *

I spent the first three years after Jon died working on a book in my head, and occasionally on paper. I think it was part of my strategy to help me get through that time. The 'book' was about men, the way they live their lives, the pressures they face, and about trying to make sense of Jon's death. Then I read Manhood by Steve Biddulph (a good and helpful read), and discovered he'd already written most of 'my' book (without the Jon parts).

So, I shelved the book plans. But fifteen years after Jon died, there now seems to be a different book to write. It still has ideas about the different ways men and women move through life, marriage or parenthood. But it is also about the life I'm living and have lived with my children and our family and friends, and how it is possible to survive and thrive through something which seems at times unsurvivable.

I am no expert. I am a social worker, and I know some useful theories about life. But if I have learned anything over fifteen years, it is that theories are fairly irrelevant in the face of reality. They can inform and lend a helpful skeleton. But winging it, hoping to get things right more often than not, and asking for help before you get desperate are all, in my experience, more real. I only know about how I've lived after my partner took his own life. For anyone who has lost a partner in the same way, I hope some of this book may speak to you, and at least make you feel you're not the only one going through the unimaginable. For others who have lost a partner under other circumstances, you might recognise some of what is here. And for anyone who's reading out of interest rather than personal experience, something here might give you a light bulb moment in how to help, or understand, a friend who is going through something like this.

When I started writing this, I thought it would be a simple process. I'd had these thoughts and memories in my head for all these years; I thought I'd made sense and come to terms with most of it. But the process has been much harder than I imagined. I've had to take time out to re-group and gather myself more than once.

Part of that has been because other bits of life have coincided and ramped up the emotional experience of doing this. And I've more than once questioned the value of trying to tell what is actually a story without an ending. It doesn't conclude with a brilliant revelation of how everything will all be all right, or that I've set up a charity to support people going through something similar. I haven't run marathons to raise funds and awareness. I've just lived my life for fifteen years, and tried to make my children's lives without their dad as positive as possible, in the only way I know how.

In retrospect, there have been real peaks and troughs during the time since Jon died. There hasn't been a pattern of steadily heading towards a light at the end of a tunnel, or reaching the peak of a seemingly unclimbable mountain. Instead, there have been times when I felt totally unassailable – when it seemed that I was juggling all the balls and holding everything together, and had boundless energy. At other times I've felt utterly desolate, sad, lonely, useless and with no clue about what to do next or how to do it. Maybe that's just life? I suspect everyone has 'phase swings' (like mood swings but longer) because life throws tough and challenging things at most of us. But my only life experience is this one which has had Jon's death behind the past fifteen years, so I've tended to put my phase swings down to that.

These ups and downs have had no rational or predictable pattern. The bad times have lessened over time, but I'd be disingenuous if I said they never happen any more. The superwoman moments have lessened too. I think, like the early plans for the original 'book', my feelings of unassailability were in direct response to the intensity of how hard life still felt in the early years, and how much I felt I had to prove – to myself, but to other people too. When I got it right, I felt like an Amazonian warrior! Had I written our story at one of those times, with fewer years of living this life under my belt and a temporarily kick-ass kind of attitude, it would have read very differently. It would have been no less a reflection of my experience, or perception of my children's experiences, but it would have been very one dimensional.

Today I feel like a more balanced person, and that I can tell our story realistically, without claiming that there was a battle to be won, and that we've been victorious. I have read many things over the years about people facing adverse and challenging situations, often only a few years or months after the traumatic event. Their stories are courageous and inspiring and often 'victorious' – but also exhausting, and with a tendency to make me feel somehow lacking. When I decided to write this account, it was because it was about the long haul, with all the little victories and defeats that are part of our everyday life without Jon.

There isn't an ending to this story. It is a work in progress. But it is about real life.

THINGS JON WAS GOOD AT

Running

Making popcorn

Gardening

Travelling

Hillwalking

Maths

Spilling baked beans down clean t-shirts

Photography

Growing bonsai trees

Making tents

Being Eilidh's dad

Rock climbing

Windsurfing

Making margaritas

Reading voraciously

Cooking (curry)

Scuba diving

Passing off others' one-liners as his own (Butch Cassidy's and the Sundance Kid's were particular favourites)

Changing nappies

Woodwork

Drawing

Skiing

Cycling

CHAPTER 1

THE EARLY MONTHS

'I Can Do This'

I didn't actually ever say that. And certainly often felt anything *other* than able to do it. But looking back, there must have been a tacit, subconscious decision somewhere deep within me that I would, and could, do it. Keep going, that is. Within the first month of Jon's death I watched a *Kilroy* show while I was breastfeeding Cameron. It was about being young and bereaved. With an odd sense of detachment, I watched and listened to the people who had been widowed at an early age and found I couldn't identify with any of them — especially the woman who said she didn't leave her house for the first month, and spent all her waking and sleeping hours wearing her deceased husband's sweatshirt and sweatpants.

I felt huge empathy for her, but I didn't understand how that would be possible. I had no choice but to get up every day, and do what the children needed me to do. Maybe I should have titled this section 'I have to do this' rather than 'I can do this'. The end result was the same, I suppose.

Two things I understand now: first, I was in shock, and my way of coping and keeping going was to keep very busy, constantly distracted and never giving myself time to think. I carried on like that for eight years. Second, grieving is a completely individual process. Theories of bereavement suggest a clear and predictable pattern of stages, acknowledging that they can be experienced in a different order and for differing lengths of time from person to person. I knew that – I'd written essays about it during my social work training.

THE FUNERAL

But the reality of grief was not like any theory I ever read. Even now, the months and years following Jon's death feel like a technicolour voyage through peaks and valleys of the most intense emotional landscape, but without a clear route through it. I wonder if whoever refers to a funeral as a means of gaining 'closure' has ever been to one for someone they loved? A funeral undoubtedly puts an end to the craziness of the first short time after a death, when all of real life is put on hold, and you seem to see the world from a great distance or height, or through a fuzzy lens, or as if you have your head under water. Our home was full of people from the day Jon died until the night of the funeral. I think friends just wanted to be close to us and their presence and practical and emotional support were wonderful – but not part of normal life. (Of course life was never going to be the old 'normal' ever again.)

A funeral, I believe, should be an occasion when everyone can be united in their loss, and express their grief openly. But it should also celebrate the person's life, even when that life was painfully short. And we did, I think, manage that for Jon, who had done so many things worth celebrating. I believe in Humanist principles and do not have a religious faith, and so did not think there was an afterlife to which Jon was going. Celebrating everything he loved and embraced during his life on earth was most important. We did have a Church of Scotland funeral service though, which I agreed to for Jon's parents' sakes. Ultimately, although the religious content meant nothing to me, I knew it would be important for them, and the eulogy given by our local minister – who I had never previously met – captured the essence of Jon and his love of life remarkably well, despite us only having a brief time to convey his story to her. I remember feeling almost apologetically sympathetic towards her, having to come into our family and make sense of such pain.

As with so much of that week after he died, I have very vivid memories of the day of Jon's funeral, although they are all seen and felt through the prism of the complete disbelief that my husband was dead, that our baby was only three weeks old, and at the age of thirty-five I was going to be the widow at his funeral. Numbness, a blessing I think, set in before we left for the crematorium, and I felt for most of the remainder of the day as if I was viewing everything from about twenty feet above the world. I didn't wear black, and neither did any of my family; and nor did a few friends, for which I was incredibly grateful. I hadn't had the presence of mind to suggest people wore colours, but I knew I wanted to remember Jon's vivacity with colour and not in black widow's weeds, and was so glad that those few friends had also felt the same. At the last minute I also knew I couldn't travel in the undertaker's limousine, and so dad drove us in his car. That didn't make our arrival at the crematorium any more bearable. Driving past the hearse waiting with Jon's coffin inside, and then past a sea of faces bereft and raw with their shock at Jon's death. Having to walk into the building, and sit at the front of the room while everyone filed in past us, the weight of grief tangible in the air. Listening to the service, to the eulogy, to the readings by friends, and unable to take my eyes from the coffin. 'Highland Cathedral' playing as we walked out – which, even now, I struggle to listen to – and then hugging or shaking hands with everyone. All the time feeling as if it couldn't be real, that this was not my life, but knowing it must be because all those people I knew were there for us.

So I suppose what the funeral achieved was the absolute public acknowledgment that Jon really was dead, and an opportunity for those who knew and loved him to share their sense of loss together. What it didn't offer was 'closure', or the stepping stone to 'moving on'. Both of those took much, much longer.

ACCEPTING HELP

We didn't have to leave our home, and nor did I ever have to work full time. In the midst of the awful thing that happened, we were lucky that Jon had a good life-insurance policy. Coping with poverty or loss of our home on top of our bereavement, as many have to do, would have been so much harder. I am grateful every day that we didn't have to face that too.

In the earliest weeks after Jon died, whenever I took the children to the park, or to the shops, or driving anywhere, doing any everyday things, there was a constant loop in my head saying 'my husband has killed himself…I am out here, looking like an average, rational person, but actually, I am screaming, and I can't really understand how this is happening'. And I felt like going up to complete strangers to say, 'my husband just died, by the way'. At the same time, and probably due to the weirdness of grief, I was revelling in having a new baby and a toddler who was full of curiosity about her world. The children were the reason I got up in the mornings, and they gave me huge joy. From the day Jon died, they have been my reason for everything I do. I'm not a schmaltzy, over-sentimental mother, but they are my absolute priorities.

What I couldn't have expressed or understood, however, was how incredibly hard it was going to be to care for them single-handed while trying to get through the early stages of my grief. My parents, though, were clear from the day after the funeral that Mum would not go home (to Cheshire) until we had managed to find someone who could help out with the crazy, tea and bedtime end of the day. They were of course quite right. Those hectic few hours at the end of a long day of caring for toddlers or babies were usually only manageable with the anticipation of the sound of the baby-sharing-other-person's key in the door. And when the key in the door didn't happen any more, it was the worst time of day to be reminded of Jon's loss.

So I soon agreed with them that an extra pair of hands would be much appreciated, and hopefully help me retain a degree of calm and control. While we searched for our girl Friday (Monday to Friday actually; and girls, as it turned out for a while), Mum stayed with us. And although those were a strange and grief-filled couple of months, and I was constantly aware of the sacrifice for her and Dad of not being together, and her not being at home living her own life, we did have lots of fun. Mum filled the gap in our family – not with a Jon-shaped piece, but in a Mum and Granny-shaped way. Her constant presence kept me from going under. And I have no doubt that she also helped to make Eilidh's transition from pedestal-dwelling only child to big sister (with her new attention-demanding baby brother) – and which for her coincided with the loss of her daddy – infinitely less painful. While I had to sit around feeding Cameron on a regular basis, Mum kept Eilidh occupied with imaginative games and stories and crafts, and would take her out whenever possible to give me a break.

Of course, as soon as I was released from feeding duties, Eilidh would squeeze every ounce of attention out of me she could. But having a full-time other person there, rather than a very part-time partner (as would have been the case had Jon still been around, but working full time) greatly helped to alleviate the maternal guilt that I suspect all parents feel most of the time, but especially in the early stages of dual (or triple) parenting. So I managed occasional moments alone with Cameron if Mum and Eilidh were out, being gooey and marvelling over his perfect baby toes, or his blissfully sunny temperament, or his obvious intelligence (from the way he absorbed all the details of his Spot the Dog book). And when they got back, I could happily hand him over to Mum and then spend some proper time playing with Eilidh, without the distraction of the baby imposter...

And Mum took a lot of the practical, boring bits of housework and cooking off my shoulders, and always gave Cameron his last feed of the evening so I could get an early night in anticipation of the multiple through-the-night feeds he seemed to need. (A small aside, for the record, although please don't quote me on this. I know you're not meant to have your baby sleep in bed with you, but when you're exhausted and bereaved and the baby is hungry, I think feeding him in your bed, and then perhaps falling asleep together is OK. Cameron was a big, bouncing baby – I don't think he was ever in danger of me not noticing I'd rolled on top of him. Small things do add up to stop you going insane.)

After a slightly shaky first attempt, we did find two young women to come and help with childcare for a couple of hours on different evenings. And Mum finally got to go home full time, only having been prepared to leave us for a couple of day's flying visit halfway through her two months with us. Although I was filled with dread about being left by myself, I knew I had to get on with real life without her constant reassurance and support, and her being the other adult person alongside me. Both of the girls we found were working in childcare already. Zoe stayed with us for a few months. Carol Ann stayed for almost three years, although latterly only coming a couple of times a week, and only because she felt like part of the family by then. She only stopped coming when she had a baby of her own.

Jon's parents were also an important part of the children's lives. Inevitably, our relationships with them have been different than with my own parents, to whom I've always been very close. My natural instinct has been to spend time with my family whenever we can, and we share details of our everyday lives. They are the people who love me and the children unconditionally and, certainly in the early years after Jon died, were my first port of call for sharing all of life's ups and downs.

From the time I first met Jon's parents, I was aware there was a tangible difference between our families – I come from a long line of huggers and comfortable sharers of emotional business (although not unnecessary dumpers of all life's stresses and niggles). In contrast, Jon's parents were much more of the keep-it-all-wrapped-up school of relationships, and in the early years they seemed to find my inclination to hug them when Jon and I visited quite odd. To be fair, Jon's dad did seem over the years to come to quite enjoy the habit, and always greeted a hug with a bluff little laugh (I could almost hear him saying, 'Oh my, here comes that woman again with her strange modern, hugging ways…'). Before the children were born we visited them quite regularly; they lived much closer to us than my own parents. And after Eilidh was born, they loved their new grandparental roles, and living nearer by, were able to offer much appreciated babysitting.

In the earliest days after Jon died, though, I actually wondered if I'd ever be able to look them in the face or speak to them again, so overwhelming was my anger towards them. In those darkest days, with Jon's painfully recent words still vivid in my head, and being in no fit state to think more rationally, I blamed them for his mental health problems. In tears of frustration the week before he died he had told me how useless he felt because his parents had 'made him' like he was, with no capacity to deal properly with his emotional life – even being scared to do so. This didn't surprise me as he'd talked about his 'stiff-upper-lip' upbringing many times before and my own experience of them had been as reserved and emotionally boundaried people. But on the day he said it, his desperation flooded me with anger against them, and with compassion for him – and immediately after Jon died, those words of his completely filled my head to such an extent that I struggled to be in the same room as his parents. In the week leading up to the funeral, thankful – in one sense – that the house was constantly full of friends and family, I'd take the chance to leave and go out for a walk with some of them, and avoid having to speak to his mum and dad.

Of course, my anger retreated remarkably quickly. I don't think it's possible to sustain that degree of irrational rage for any length of time without having some kind of internal emotional meltdown, and I'm also not usually a red mist kind of person. Once those feelings began to lessen, there was space for me to consider Jon's parents' own pain at his loss, and I started to gain a more balanced perspective.

And of course, his frustration with what he perceived as his emotionally repressed upbringing was only one element of all the things I knew had built up to his decision to take his own life. Although their power was overwhelming at the time, his words were nevertheless those of a deeply troubled person who was not in a rational frame of mind. I was also increasingly aware of his parents' pain, and guilt that their son had chosen to leave all of us to cope alone without him; and I think, at that point, they genuinely believed I might try and exclude them from our lives. I had no intention of doing so and realised that it would be important for the children to have a relationship with their grandparents, if we could all allow that to happen. A couple of weeks after the funeral, when his folks were visiting at the end of the day, having still been finding it hard to be anything much more than civil with them, I asked his mum if she'd like to help bathe Cameron. I can still picture the look of what I took to be gratitude and relief on her face when I did so, and I knew that no matter what I felt about their relationship with Jon in the past, they would want to be a part of their grandchildren's lives, and I would do what I could to enable them to be so.

Despite this, and my perception of them as emotionally reserved people, I have never doubted that Jon's parents loved Eilidh and Cameron. I also have no doubt that they loved Jon and his brother, and were proud and supportive parents – they were no different to any number of people of their generation, raising their children in the way they thought best, even if what I regarded as emotional openness eluded them. I knew, too, that Jon's upbringing had been a happy one, despite the emotional restraint.

In return, I know Jon loved his parents, albeit he was at times confounded by them. In the months following Jon's death, watching his parents try to make sense of the unbearable thing that their son had chosen to do, I was struck by the courage with which they faced this. I know that they must have had many painful and searching conversations with each other and they displayed unexpected insight into the aspects of their relationship with Jon that should have been more open. Sometime after he died they acknowledged to me that they rarely if ever expressed their love for their boys in simple and clear words, and admitted that expressing any emotions did not come easily to them. To make this connection between Jon's upbringing and his psychological and emotional make-up must have taken significant soul-searching for them, and I respected them for it.

It seemed that the time and effort they put into their shared time with Eilidh and Cameron was partly to make amends for this. They were loving and attentive with them, and found lots of activities they could share when the children were young. Both avid readers, they often read stories with them, Jon's dad especially. Being practical and creative, he also made models with them – monster trucks out of cardboard and wooden Roman shields and axes as Cameron got older. He had begun to teach him the basics of wood working before he died in 2009, and they often went to the beach together for serious sandcastle building. Jon's mum did baking with both children when they were little, and tried to teach Eilidh to knit on more than one occasion. She and Cameron have fond memories of these shared experiences, and I greatly appreciated the breaks they afforded me at the time.

Jon's mum still lives quite near to us and we see her quite regularly. While there were long periods when I found it hard to understand what I perceived as the emotional distance she kept from us – in spite of my efforts to broach this – in more recent times she has seemed much more open, and keen to have contact. This has felt like a real enrichment for all of us. She loves the children, and I know she has enjoyed the girlyness of having a granddaughter after parenting two boys and having two grandsons. While she does not understand why I felt the need to write this book, I admired her courage in reading it, and I hope it has given her a new insight into the children's and my experiences over the past fifteen years.

CHAPTER 2

A CRASH COURSE IN WIDOWED SINGLE PARENTING

So yes, in those earliest weeks and months I did 'do it', and found a way to make the time pass, with lots of help from other people. But the long haul was round the corner, and if I thought the early stages were challenging, there was much more to come.

For a long time I wanted to run away. Or get in the car and drive without stopping. Not to get away from the children...nothing so specific. Just a nebulous but overwhelming urge to not be in this – to not be responsible for everything, to not have to keep coping with it all, *all the time*. But I knew I wouldn't, because it wasn't an option. Confoundingly, there were huge amounts of joy mixed in with the exhaustion and relentlessness. I felt strong and proud at times when things were going well for the three of us, when we were having fun doing things together – although that was always tainted by a wish that Jon could be sharing it all with us. But whenever the children did something funny or clever I'd think, 'Wow! They're mine!' and the gorgeousness of that wave of love always made up for the harder stuff.

But it *was* hard. I felt bone tired for years, from being responsible for everything but also from carrying the weight of Jon's loss. I fantasised about getting off the endless loop of caring and knowing and cleaning and sorting everything: of having to be the goodie and the baddie all the time, and feeling frustrated for the children that they had to make sense of my spilt personality. I did manage very occasional tiny breaks, a few weekends away with different girlfriends over the years – blissful, escapist weekends while Mum and Dad poured everything into having lovely times with the children. And because I trusted them so completely, and knew the children were having a wonderful, indulgent, Granny and Grandpa-made jolly, I switched off from everything. And I relished the time with my friends, revelled in it. Felt reconnected with my non-mum self.

But going home was always difficult. When Mum and Dad left, the suddenness of just being the three of us again was stark and I found my aloneness hard to bear. I know I wasn't absolutely alone. But the other grown-up person who was meant to be sharing our experiences wasn't there, and his absence felt especially raw at those times. Coming home from trips away with the children was the same – returning home to the empty house by ourselves, the unpacking and sorting to do, and the children small and tired and needing my attention and love and patience. For years, I hated having to face those times. But as with every part of life, they became bearable, and then fine, and then just normal. All the challenging aspects of our life since Jon died were like this. Dark or scary or overwhelming. And for a long time I couldn't imagine how they would ever feel better.

But they did, and do. I worried for years about things going wrong during the night – the children both getting sick at the same time and having to deal with it. An emergency happening with one of them, and what would I do with the other?

What happened was that I just dealt with it. They did both get sick at the same time, as young children do. Lots of laundry. Lots of mopping up. Not much sleep. Not ideal, but survivable. And there weren't many emergencies, thankfully. The most pressing happened when they were both a bit older, and I needed to take Cameron to the hospital quite late at night. Eilidh insisted on coming too because she would only have worried if she didn't, but I had a friend on call if she decided to go home to her bed. I have learnt that people are quite happy to help if you just ask them.

So we just got used to our new 'everyday'. I worked out ways of dealing with different challenges. The children grew up and became less physically needy and immediately demanding of my attention all the time. Time passed. But in the early months and years I felt as if I was clinging to control of my life by my fingertips, and it took very little to throw me off balance completely.

CLINGING ON TO CONTROL

I had worked out what I needed to do to feel in control, and to cope with the things I needed to do every day – the boring bits, and the fun bits with the children. I've always been organised, but I took it to a different level. All small children enjoy and thrive in a clear and predictable routine but I needed it, too, to keep my sanity intact. If everything went according to plan, I was fine. But unexpected events threw me completely, and not just into a sense of disorganisation, but right back into the deepest grief and panic that Jon wasn't there.

The most difficult times were when friends (with or without children) were around – either us visiting them, or them visiting us. As with so many experiences in those early years, these were double-edged swords. I loved spending time with friends, and having the normality of life with them and our young children. But I was only just keeping on top of what I needed to do with Eilidh and Cameron every day, so feeding or accommodating extra people for a weekend, or tidying up the mess of four or six children's playtime, instead of just two, required a big effort of will, and I suspect the tension I felt was visible for all to see.

Equally challenging – or exciting? – was trying to deal with Eilidh's occasionally unpredictable and always inquisitive behaviour. I remember one visit to friends who didn't have children. I became aware that I hadn't seen her for a few minutes, and, leaving Cameron with the friends, went to look for her. In the space of those few short minutes, Eilidh had managed to get the childproof lid (all parents know there really is no such thing) off the toilet cleaner (child-free people have no need to keep them in out-of-the-way-cupboards) and cover the bathroom floor with it (but thankfully not drink it), and then made her way upstairs where she found all the carefully organised and filed photographs, which she had emptied out of all their envelopes into a mountainous pile on the floor. Similarly, on other occasions she spread Sudocrem all over a friend's bedroom wall and floor, spilled nail varnish on another friend's brand-new carpet, and emptied cornflakes and eggs on another friend's kitchen floor. (Cornflakes and eggs all cleanable. Sudocrem and nail varnish less so.) She also went through a phase of biting other little children (which had me shadowing her round soft play centres and parks like a shifty MI5 agent, ready to remove her as soon as she bared her teeth). And I caught her just in time to stop her pulling a friend's baby off the bed where he'd been having his nappy changed.

None of these were very different to things she'd done before Jon died and are probably familiar to many parents of toddlers. Mostly, they were pretty funny, in retrospect (well, not the nail varnish incident, or the baby on the bed). But at the time, they were the straws to break my camel's back on more than one occasion. Because grief does strange things to us – and a fragile grasp on the control of reality is one of them. I think, too, that because I was so desperately trying to be the best possible parent, every time something breached my defences, it felt like a terrible failure. What I couldn't see then was that I was trying to be two parents at once, making a fairly good job of it, but being overwhelmed by Jon's absence.

Of course, it wasn't just me who was missing Jon. Eilidh undoubtedly felt his loss too. How much of her behaviour in the earliest years was a result of her grief, or just average toddler and child behaviour, I don't know. It doesn't really matter, because it still had to be handled carefully. And I felt a huge sense of responsibility to try and get it right and single-handedly set her on a positive path (and not the continuing path of hooliganism she sometimes seemed bent on).

I'll talk about how the children have been affected by the loss of their dad in more detail later, but there are two things which I'll mention here: how to stop the older child attempting to injure the younger child, and potty training.

PROTECTION AND POTTIES

Avoiding injury to the baby quickly became a priority. I don't know if it was because Eilidh felt supplanted by Cameron like many older siblings do, or whether it was made worse by the simultaneous loss of her daddy, but she regularly found potential weapons to use against him. Anything with a bit of heft to it — books, toys, long poky sticks for when he was in his cot. All were actually quite easy to deal with: constant vigilance to ensure all such objects were out of her reach, as constant as possible distraction with creative and entertaining pastimes and, when push came to shove, a lock beyond her reach on Cameron's door so I could put him safely down for naps in his cot. That worked for as long as it took her to realise she could drag a chair and climb up to reach it. The first time I discovered she could do that was when I had gone in to get him up from a nap and she locked us both in. She then resisted my numerous enticements to unlock it, so I eventually had to use my not insignificant mama-bear frustration-induced force to burst the lock open.

That signalled the end of the door-locking period. Soon afterwards Eilidh seemed to stop wanting to hurt Cameron, and in fact went through a very cute phase of climbing into his cot with him to cuddle him or read him a story. Short-lived, as all childhood phases are in retrospect, but cute while it lasted.

Potty training was a longer process. Jon and I tried to start it with Eilidh before Cameron was born, thinking it would make life easier to have only one set of nappies to deal with at a time. Eilidh took no interest whatsoever. We decided to shelve the plan for a few months.

Shortly after Jon died, being in the 'I must keep doing all the things we planned and be two parents rolled into one' phase, I tried again. Eilidh was not quite two-and-a-half. I'd read the books. I'd spoken with our health visitor. I knew the theory. We read the children's books together about how much fun using a potty was. Still she showed no interest whatsoever.

I'd suggest taking her nappy off for a while so she could play, and then let me know when she wanted to go on the potty. She wee'd on the duvet. Or on the sofa. Or anywhere, except on the potty. She was a smart little girl: I had no doubt after trying this for a while that she was telling me in no uncertain terms to back off. Her daddy was gone, I was still putting nappies on the imposter baby, and she was meant to grow up and wear pants instead? Not likely. On top of which, cleaning up after her fell into the category of things which lessened my control on life. So I shelved the plan again. Life was too short to be doing something which was stressful for both of us.

As it turned out, Eilidh was out of nappies by the time she was three. It just happened when she was ready. It may have been a bit later than scheduled, or recommended, but schedules and recommendations aren't really there for children and parents who have lost a major person in their lives. Being in nappies until you're nearly three doesn't mean you're neglected or under-stimulated or any other thing that will make your parent feel guilty – and it won't, I promise, harm your life chances. Please feel free to apply this theory to many other aspects of child rearing. If you know you have your children's best interests at heart, and they are safe and loved and cared for, bending the rules and recommendations, in my experience, is really OK.

MISSING JON – MISSING DADDY

Single parenting is hard, whatever the circumstances leading to it: it's tough being the only adult when the door closes behind you at night, and being responsible for everything, all the time, never having anyone else to say 'Be nice to Mummy, she's tired' or 'Just do what you're told.' And it is made worse by your knowledge that in most houses there are 'normal' families, with two parents sharing the load. And so you gird up your loins, again, to be upbeat and have fun and keep the children cheery while the tea gets made, and think of wholesome, creative games to play before bath time – all the while knowing there's no way of escaping the house that night, to nip to the coffee shop, or for a gym class, or anything that doesn't involve the children. The fact that Jon took his own life only added another dimension of loneliness to all of this lone parenting.

And the world is full of daddies when you don't have one. The Botanic Gardens in Edinburgh, one of our favourite hang-outs for adventures and hide and seek and illicit picnics when the children were young, was over-populated by happy, two-parent families every weekend. Weekdays were safer, when most of the dads tended to be at work. But weekends were family time – proper families, with the proper number of parents. And even as a little girl Eilidh was painfully aware of it, often telling me she didn't like to be there because of all the daddies. I could see her observing what the 'proper' families did together, could feel the sadness and the anger exuding from her little person, and I felt so useless that I couldn't make it better for her.

It was different for Cameron, who had no memories of his daddy, and who had had so little time with him here. Eilidh had very clear memories, which I've made sure she knows were her memories, and not things I have reminded her about: sitting down beside Jon after he came in from a run (but wise enough, even at two, not to sit on his knee because he was so sweaty), sitting with him on the sofa eating out of a huge bowl of popcorn, riding on his shoulders, sitting in the seat on the back of his bike (and falling asleep against his back). I have a huge sadness for Cameron that he has no memories of Jon, and I know the loss and pain he and Eilidh feel are different because of this. He has no memories. She has all her memories until the age of 27 months.

The world continues to be full of dads, and partners. It has never become something I don't think about, but for the last few years, it has no longer been the raw wound which I felt would never heal. We've been a team of three for all but two weeks of our 15 years of family life together. It's been our usual for a very long time, although I remember thinking when the children were young that our family felt somehow unbalanced with only one parent for two children. It seemed unfair for them. But once Eilidh was five years old, she had lived more of her life without her dad than with him, and we're 12 years on from that now. Time doesn't really heal, but it has given me the chance to get used to things being the way they are.

But, a small wise word to bereaved single parents. Just because you feel less profoundly grief stricken or sad as time passes, it doesn't mean there aren't days when, like anyone else, you feel completely knackered, your resistance and tolerance are down – and then the children push your buttons. First, you have to deal with that without anyone else to bail you out or back you up, while also trying not to lose your rag and emotionally scar the children for life (there's that parental guilt again). But second, it can also fling you right back in the face of your loss and your single parent-ness even though it may have been weeks, or months, since that last happened.

Fifteen years on, these experiences are few and far between. The children push very different buttons these days. My ability to deal with them, and their ability to respond like rational young adults, are hugely improved, and I think that any emotional crossroads or dilemmas facing me are as much a result of being 50, and what's going on in our various life stages, rather than any residual loss and mourning issues. That's not to say there aren't occasional days when I still scream to myself in frustration at having to manage everything by myself, and there being no partner to say, 'How was your day? How are you doing? Can I do something to help?' (Oh, the fantasy of some volunteered help!) But to be honest, it's rare, and likely to be common to many parents of teens.

GOING BACK TO WORK

In the early years, though, when grief and parental guilt still went hand in hand, there were constant dilemmas, and how to balance work and being with the children was a big one. I enjoyed my job – I'd worked for years as a social worker in fostering and adoption services. Going back to work after maternity leave with Cameron reconnected me with my old self. I could be the working person, not just the widowed mum of two little children – although, of course, all my colleagues and carers were incredibly kind and careful and solicitous, so it didn't feel quite like the old working me.

After a few months, it also started to feel stressful. Not the work itself, but the juggling of the children's needs at both ends of the day, and trying to make the transition from work-mum to home-mum without losing my patience with them when we were all tired. I felt as if I couldn't meet all their needs and keep working as I was, without losing more of my sense of control. My desperation to feel I was on top of everything combined with feeling constantly guilty that I wasn't around enough for Cameron and Eilidh began to be overwhelming.

And I just missed them when I wasn't with them. I kept asking myself what I would do if, five years down the line, having kept working as I was, we were all stressed, and I had messed up my relationships with the children because I hadn't been emotionally and physically available for them. Feeling out of control, and exacerbating my own grief, was bad enough. But I was determined not to become a stressed parent, working too much, and not being there to respond to my children's grief or other needs whenever they needed me to. I was all too aware of the emotional damage which children could experience if their attachments to their most important carers were disrupted in any way.

A LITTLE BIT OF THEORY

'Attachment' is the theoretical term which describes the relationships between babies, children and their care-givers. A baby naturally seeks to be close to a care-giver who can provide security or comfort, and they do this by signalling their needs usually through crying, reaching out or crawling towards their carer. They may be hungry, or tired, or need changing, or just want a cuddle, but before they can speak, crying is the most effective attention grabber. If the care-giver responds appropriately and lovingly to these 'attachment behaviours', the baby's stress will be relieved and they will feel emotionally secure. The more this positive cycle of interactions occurs, the more secure the baby will feel. A baby's healthy exploration of, and discovery about, their world can only take place from an emotionally secure base. Subsequent healthy, normal child development can only take place if this secure base is in place from the earliest stages of babyhood.

If a care-giver's responses are unpredictable, erratic or non-existent, and a secure attachment isn't developed, the impact on a child may be severe and last throughout their childhood. A child who is 'insecurely' attached – and, crucially, doesn't have the chance to build strong attachments with any other care-givers – may display a range of behaviours including poor attention span, low self-esteem, difficulty expressing feelings, confused thought processes, behaviour or emotions similar to those following bereavement, and generally 'challenging' behaviours. My professional knowledge has often been helpful in my personal life, but as an already guilt-ridden single parent, my experience of working with children who were living with the consequences of insecure early-years attachments served specifically to harden my resolve to spend as much time as possible with Eilidh and Cameron.

I was very fortunate that I could choose to leave my job at that time, given that we had a financial cushion from Jon's work pension. I became a freelance social worker instead, which meant I could work flexibly around the children's schedules, and I have continued to do this for the past 14 years. I've been able to work more or fewer hours depending on the time of year, so I've been lucky never to have had to deal with the juggling act of arranging holiday childcare like so many people have to – a logistical headache even with two parents. And I have never regretted making that decision. I have no doubt I've not always got things right in parenting my children, but at least I can only blame myself for that, and not the fact that I chose to work longer hours when I didn't have to.

SUPPORT – WHEN TO ACCEPT
AND WHEN TO LET GO

The other thing for which I have never stopped being grateful has been the support of our friends and family. My need for this has changed over the years. Nowadays, if someone does an unexpected kind thing or makes a caring gesture of help, it's lovely and always appreciated, but no longer because it is helping to prevent me from falling into the abyss. In the first two or three years, they may not have known it, but that was undoubtedly the case. I was able to keep doing all the things I was doing – having fun with the children, caring for all their needs, running the house, planning our lives, working, and managing to spend time with friends – but only thanks to the scaffolding provided by the almost constant attention from the people who loved us best. Mostly, that was Mum and Dad, but friends were, and many still are, also a major part of our lives and support network.

In the earliest months, we were rarely alone in the evenings. Old family friends and one work colleague in particular regularly dropped in to keep us company and to help out with the children's bedtime routines. Eilidh was obsessed with women's handbags at that stage, and used to greet people at the door by demanding, 'I have your bag now!', to such an extent that one friend of Mum's filled a 'fake' bag with all sorts of interesting things so it could be safely abducted without risk to keys or phone or any really vital items. And everyone was kind in all sorts of other ways. They brought story books for the children to read before bedtime, played endless imaginative games with them while I got on with boring but necessary jobs and were just there to be another grown-up person alongside me.

As the first year wore on, though, after one too many enquiries from Eilidh of 'who's coming tonight, Mummy?' and feeling too as if our house wasn't really our own any more, I thanked everyone for their love and support, but asked if they could give us some space. I had to try and create a new normality at home. As when Mum left us after the first two months, I felt torn between needing to run my own life again, but also knowing it would mean being thrust up against the loneliness so much more. It was a milestone that I needed to pass, and it was hard, but like everything, it got easier. And it did become our new ordinary.

Friends continued to offer big and small kindnesses for years – from unexpectedly dropping in some home-cooked food for our dinner or picking up shopping to save me going out with both children, to planning and organising weekends away together, so we could just drop in to a ready-made mini holiday. I know that many of them re-arranged their weekend or holiday or New Year plans so that they could be with us instead, and those gestures were and still are hugely appreciated. As the children got older, some of our best friends had Eilidh and Cameron to stay for the night while I went off and reconnected my non-mum self with other friends. At times when I felt I couldn't do more than struggle through everyday life, the spirit of love with which those gestures were given made all the difference between coping and not. At the time, I was grateful, but looking back, I also realise how much thought friends put in to how best to show us their love and care. The power of practical gestures should never be underestimated – hugs and a sympathetic ear were and are always valuable. But a friend's love that went into baking a cake, or taking charge of a day trip to somewhere for an adventure or an escape from reality was often a sanity-saver.

And my mum and dad and sister Julia: I would not have survived intact without them (and even with them, I still crumbled a few years down the line). We are lucky to have the love and friendship of many people, but I know my parents and sister completely and unconditionally care about us. In the early years, I relied very heavily on them – not by expecting them to be with us all the time, or telling them how I felt at every junction of the bereavement path. But the knowledge that they were metaphorically walking that path alongside us, and shoring us up with their love and care provided me with a tangible emotional safety net.

Before my parents moved back to Scotland, about a year after Jon's death, they lived four hours' journey away from us, but since then, they have been less than an hour-and-a-half distant, which means we can visit each other easily, but not feel as if we are living in each other's pockets. In the very earliest months, I allowed myself to be mopped up by them. Anything they offered to do, times they came to visit, anything they wanted to do with the children – I accepted it all, willingly, gladly, gratefully. They took over wherever I left off, and they knew exactly what needed doing with the children, or the housework, or our lives. It was a physical, emotional and practical relief to hand all of that over to them for a couple of days every now and then. I didn't so much recharge my batteries at those times – they were so depleted, that would have taken considerably longer, and I knew I couldn't give myself up quite so completely to that process – but the presence of my parents, exuding love for us, was the best balm for my exhausted and devastated spirit.

I also loved being able to share the children with them. Over the past 15 years there has never been a brilliant thing they have done or achieved that I haven't wished Jon could have been here for. And I mean everything: every paint-splodged picture, crazy autumn leaf rummaging at the Botanics, adventures in the countryside and at old castles, learning to tie shoelaces and school ties, climbing Munros, making me laugh, getting angry about injustices in the world, getting prizes at school. But Mum, Dad and Julia have been the receptacles for the joy and pride from all those amazing things alongside Eilidh, Cameron and me. And Mum and Dad especially have been with us to do most of them, too. Even when I still wore my grief badly disguised as 'coping-just-fine', we had lots of fun. Whatever I planned to do with the children, Mum and/or Dad did too if they were visiting. I didn't relinquish all responsibility – it was just good to have someone to share it with who understood everything.

I gained a dawning realisation, however, as the months passed, that Mum had put her own arrangements on hold. The penny dropped after they had moved back to Scotland and I was asking if they had made plans to go back and visit friends in Cheshire. After a couple of conversations where she evaded the subject, or made

39

paltry excuses for not being able to arrange it, I asked why not, and she admitted that she wanted to keep her diary free 'in case we needed them'. My initial reaction was frustration. In fact, even after thinking about it for a while I was still frustrated. At that point I think I had only had to ask them for help in an emergency on one occasion, when I got a virulent tummy bug and couldn't look after the children. Any other time we saw each other was a planned visit, which admittedly provided huge support for us, but which I thought were also just regular family visits like regular families made to each other.

Now, I had an image in my mind of Mum (Dad seemed less guilty of this!) sitting at home, hovering by the phone, just waiting for something to go wrong, and leaping into action to rescue us. I was frustrated because I'd thought I was making quite a good effort of holding it all together and felt that maybe that wasn't the case after all – but much more exasperating was the fact that she was not getting on with her own life. So I told her so. In what seemed a nice and kind way, I hope. I needed to say it a few more times over the next few months – or maybe years – (along the lines of 'for goodness sake, Mother, get on with your own life!') as she found it a hard habit to break. But she did eventually manage it.

When we had those conversations, part of what was going on for me was like all the previous transition times since Jon had died – a need to reclaim my life with Cameron and Eilidh for the three of us, while simultaneously feeling panic at the prospect of losing a bit of our safety net. But at each stage of feeling able to handle more of life by myself, I knew it had to be done. What I didn't recognise so readily then was that it wasn't just us who had been bereaved. I understood that everyone else had also lost Jon, whatever their relationship with him had been. Like us, they had lost the future version of us as a family of four. And for those people who cared most about us, I know that every time they saw us without Jon it was a harsh reminder of the gap he had left in our lives. While part of that was about missing him, it was also about feeling the pain of us having to live a very different life than the one we had planned together. For my parents especially, the way they handled that was to try and do anything in their power to make things easier for us. And from this great distance of 15 years, all I think now is how wonderful that was (and continues to be). As the bereaved person, part of what you may need to do is allow people to help you, and cope with their own bereavement, in whatever way feels best for them – so long as it isn't detrimental to them or you, obviously. Because they will, for the most part, be doing it out of love and concern.

COPING WITH COMPANY

For years, friends here at home babysat for us, when I could never return the favour of night-time sitting for their children – and although my social life wasn't exactly buzzing, being able to go out always reconnected me with my adult life beyond the home, and I appreciated it greatly. Having said that, parties and gatherings were, and actually still are, a double-edged sword. I'm sociable and love being with friends. But even now, part of me feels exhausted by – usually – being the only widowed or even single person there. I'm blessed, and I suspect statistically odd, to have lots of married and coupled friends who are still in that state after up to 25 years of togetherness; but it does mean a distinct lack of other singles in my social circles.

I remember being struck in the early months after Jon died by how I suddenly saw all our male friends in a very different light than before. I had to relate directly to them, and not with Jon as a buffer. At that stage, in big groups, guys talked most often to guys and women to women. Now I had to talk to everyone. And I remember feeling as if I was a page laid bare – possibly because everyone was being kind and attentive, but also because I no longer had the validation of myself that came from being in a partnership. Not that Jon and I stood about at parties holding hands and hanging on each other's scintillating conversation. But there was a subconscious reassurance in knowing he was there, somewhere in the crowd. Suddenly, I was just me, and whatever that *me* was, I was completely responsible for all of it. And socialising in mixed company felt exhausting. Really, honestly, physically exhausting. I had to fire myself up in anticipation of going out, and convince myself that going out was better than not going out. The first party I went to, six months after Jon died, with two of my best friends as 'scaffolding', I managed one-and-a-half hours. I slapped on a smile, made small talk, did some Ceilidh dancing. That was enough. It was physically painful, mostly in my heart. But the whole effort of looking and behaving like an ordinary person was huge. And I felt far from being an ordinary person.

That was how all social gatherings were, more or less, for a long time. Gradually, I enjoyed them more than just survived them. And now, I honestly enjoy them, and going alone to parties is what I've done for much longer than I ever went as part of a couple with Jon. But going to any event still requires having to take a subconscious deep breath beforehand, and there is a pressure to be on form, when there's no one else to make excuses for you.

We've had some great holidays with friends and our family over the years. When the children were younger it was so much easier to go away with other people, because supervising, entertaining and caring for two small people alone isn't always the best of breaks from reality. Having other grown-ups around made for extra pairs of hands and some adult sanity, conversation and activity. Most often we went for long weekends, occasionally for a bit longer. They were fun times – everyone pitched in together, and it often made me think living in a commune might be worth trying… But in reality, two or three days were about as much as I could manage, for much the same reason as I found parties so hard, and also because I began to crave the safety and security of our home routine.

In 2008, we went on a two-week holiday to Crete with two other families, all close friends, one of whom had arranged the trip. We stayed in two villas high in the hills in the middle of the island, with views down the valley and swimming pools and a blessed breeze to combat the incredible heat. We visited Greek ruins, sights and beaches, ate fabulous Greek food, read and chatted ravenously. Two of us got chatted up by the oldest Greek man we'd ever seen. We watched the ceiling lamps spin in an earthquake. The children made hilarious home videos and grew fins from hours spent in the water. It was a brilliant holiday. But it was so much harder than I would ever have believed. Other holidays or mini-breaks had been just that: mini. Short and manageable so I could get out of potential trouble before it started. I hadn't, therefore, spent more than a few days at once in the company of coupled-up friends. I could parachute in to a weekend away, soak up some communal fun, a big group of people all mucking in together, and leave relatively unscathed.

By the end of the first week in Crete, though, I was reminded of what life with a partner was actually like. A long holiday allows for chilling out, taking time over things, space for little intimacies and the relaxation that everyone looks forward to in a vacation. None of my friends were in the first throes of romance. All married for at least ten years at that point, they were just going about their normal, everyday relationships. They'd check out how each other was doing, maybe put sun cream on for each other, offer to do helpful little chores. And I was brought up hard against what I had missed out on for the past seven years. They made plans for the day ahead between them, and I caught up with them as we were getting ready to leave. The dads played rough and tumble games in the pool with the children. They were all just everyday, usual things – but those are the stuff of life, and seeing it all happen before me was like watching an old film of what our lives should have been like, too. So, a week in, I had a bit of a meltdown. My friend Charlotte was wonderfully understanding, and allowed me to cry messily and wetly over her. And I let out all the pain and loneliness that I knew was there, but had been barricaded in until I was reminded of what life with four instead of three should have been.

Holidays have been fine since then. I've never been away with friends for more than a week at a time, and mostly, we have been by ourselves for the past few years. Time passing has helped – this really is our normal now. And I also know how to anticipate the couple stuff that will be part of any trip with other families.

BEING ALONE

Loneliness has still been a fairly regular companion during the last 15 years, regardless of however much time we've spent with friends and family – the lack-of-a-soul-mate lonely, not the lacking in company or activity kind. At different stages it has been for different reasons. I know that in the early years, beyond the obvious gap that Jon had left in our lives, I often struggled with memories of the more difficult times between us and felt very alone in trying to deal with them. When he was alive I never told anyone about the difficulties we had. It was our situation to deal with. After Jon died, I felt it would have been disloyal to share the memories of those times with any of our friends. But for quite long periods of time, I got stuck in quagmires where I could only recall the difficult times, when he had been cold, or dismissive, or told lies to or about me, and played what I can recognise now as mind games. The wisdom of hindsight has allowed me to rationalise those behaviours as part of his mental health problems, but being stuck reliving the feelings they engendered was as painful as it had been in real life, with the added layers of grief – and I felt unable to share any of that with anyone else, because it felt like a betrayal of him.

Those phases did always pass, and the more balanced memories of Jon took their place. The reality was that living with someone with significant mental health issues was always going to be an emotional fireworks show – some glorious, beautiful explosions and thrills, some scary and powerful ones. And the way we travel through grief and mourning means those fireworks get replayed in unpredictable and challenging ways. In more recent years, I have shared more of what life with him was really like with friends who knew him well. They know too about the loneliness which creeps or pops up, provoked by random things – being in big gatherings, not having someone (other than me) to tell the children to get up and do something to help, or not having someone to share a sofa night with. I've been able to do this, I think, because I don't feel the need to prove anything any more. I'm not always strong or unassailable, and I don't mind admitting it. I'm mostly having a great time, and feel I know what I'm doing – but I'm also occasionally vulnerable, knackered and fed up. Some of that is about everyday life. Some of it is still to do with being here without Jon. What has changed is my preparedness to admit it, and to know that no one will think any less of me if I do.

TOP TIPS FOR KEEPING IT TOGETHER

Set achievable goals and plans. Do this early on (weeks, months, first few years; everyone's early on is different). You'll feel good when you manage to get there, and it'll keep you distracted. Later, try going with the flow a bit more – the need to keep busy is less, because the grief will hopefully be less. Be kind to yourself whichever path you take.

You don't have to be perfect. Not anywhere near it. Don't beat yourself up if you don't do everything that's on your to-do list. If you are a parent, nothing, literally, is more important than spending the best times possible with your children. Cleaning their shoes, preparing complicated home-cooked meals every day, being on the nursery committee – none of them really matter.

Spend time with your children, individually. This will mean asking someone else for help. It's OK to do that. Eilidh loved it when we very occasionally managed to have some time by ourselves without Cameron. He was always much sunnier and happy-go-lucky, and just loved his big sister. He really did.

Deal with troublesome toddler behaviour. If you can find a trusted friend or family person (preferably without their own children) to help out and share the load, great. Pre-empt the challenging behaviours you know might be possible – distract with anything more exciting: games, a walk to the park, TV time, food. Have options at your fingertips before you reach a crisis point.

Get organised. In fact be super-organised with everything, but only if it doesn't stress you out. As much as possible, plan ahead so you don't get panicked by unexpected things. For example, if you have a full body-painting session before bath time, how will you get two paint-covered children from the kitchen downstairs through the house and upstairs to the bathroom without Jackson Pollocking every inch of floor and wall on the way? Apply the same principles to making car or plane travel or supermarket shopping trips fun or at least bearable. As there's not another adult person there, you have to be able to stop the toddlers getting fractious on a long journey (because it will make you stressed, too, and remind you that you're doing it alone). So have story and song tapes, or a lengthy repertoire of songs to sing at your fingertips in the car, have travel-sized games, toys and drawing materials on a plane, along with over-generous amounts of snacks. Use the early plane-boarding service for small children. Practise collapsing and folding buggies single-handed (i.e. with one hand, not just by yourself). Let the children pull their own suitcase as soon as they're big enough. And when you come home from an away trip, have a plan for keeping the children occupied immediately – make sure they have food and entertainment. (I see a theme developing here.)

Ask friends or family for help if you can. They will want to help; they may just not be sure what to do for the best. Tell them. If you need some time to yourself to go for a coffee or a bottle of wine with friends, or to do some exercise, or to garden with sharp implements (not safe with small children about), or to do your favourite thing that reminds you of the old you, that's what you need to ask them to help with. And tell them when you are feeling bad. They won't think less of you for it.

Ignore the midnight voices. If you wake in the middle of the night with your head full of stuff, listen to the radio, read a book, write a new to-do list – anything except listening to your head. Lack of sleep will bring you down hard.

Keep things simple for the children. There are bound to be times which by necessity will be hectic and add some craziness. Birthdays, for example, with heaps of presents (people tend to be very generous to children who have lost a parent), lots of extra friends and family around and excesses of sugar, can create monsters out of even the most easy-going children. A few days of simple, calm and spend-no-money time (what I used to call mooching and pootling time) – playing on the beach, going to the park, having a picnic, doing jigsaws, painting – can work wonders for everyone's over-stimulated spirits.

Take stock. If you feel, after some time, that you should be feeling a bit better but you're not, take a step back and think whether that's a usual part of grieving (see Chapter 4) or if you're falling into something deeper and harder to get out of. If it feels like the deeper, harder place, ask for professional help. (See the appendix at the end of the book.)

ADVICE TO FRIENDS

Please keep inviting your widowed (or otherwise single) friends to dinner parties. In my experience, bereaved or divorced singles are suddenly cast out of that weekend social circle and it's hard to get back into it. (I make a distinction between dinner parties and other gatherings. Somehow, invitations to big parties aren't restricted in the same way.) But, as Bridget Jones suggested in the first film, we don't have scales under our clothes (or two heads, or any other undesirable physical weirdness). And while I can't speak for everyone, the risk of us making a pass at husbands, wives or partners is negligible. Our social skills and good manners don't disappear just because our partner died. And we still quite enjoy getting out and being in the social world, having some chat or putting the world to rights. The NB is that (like everyone) there may be good days and bad for your bereaved friend, even after the shocked and wading-through-treacle early days and months have receded, so invitations may be graciously refused. But, until told otherwise, please keep trying.

WRITING IT DOWN

In the earliest years I kept a diary. A wise friend suggested it might help. It wasn't a regular thing. Looking back at it, there are gaps of months when I didn't write anything, and I never managed two days in a row. But it was a haven, and a repository for all the things I couldn't say to anyone else, and a way of letting the scream inside my head find a release valve.

When I read it now, and remembering writing it at the time, I know it was completely honest and truthful. There was no reason for it not to be. It has helped while I've been writing this to read the details of how I felt at different times in the early years. And I smiled when I read an entry in early 2003 which said, regarding my feeling of being overwhelmed at Christmas time that 'next year I'll do it differently'. Well, that never happened. And every year I still say, 'it'll be different next year' – always for different reasons, but always because I try to cram too much in, usually a work deadline, trying to make Christmas the best ever for the children, cleaning the house from top to bottom, making handmade presents for everyone. I've actually decided that I just have to live with the consequences now, because no amount of telling myself I can buy the food at M&S, nobody cares if the house is clean, and that the report can wait till January will make me behave any differently. At the age of 50, I think this is what acceptance of Christmas madness looks like.

I have a history of diary-writing but my teenage diaries were another matter altogether. Even while I was writing them, I had a fear at the back of my head that someone might find them, which would be mortifying. So my diary version of events was always more noble, and less concerned with trivia (boys) than the reality. And I made sure that when there was something really emotional (boys) going on, I'd write in real ink, so when I cried over it, the writing would get blurred. Seriously.

And I kept holiday scrapbook diaries. I voluntarily produced these until I was about 11 years old. Again: seriously? I filled them with wrappers from foreign (so much more glamorous) chewing gum and sugar cubes; matchbooks from restaurants in France where my sister and I only ever ate roast chicken and chips; and postcards. I don't think I wrote anything profound. Just gathered armfuls of stuff and stuck it in. I assumed Eilidh and Cam would be equally keen: but after a couple of half-hearted 'let's humour Mum' efforts, I stopped suggesting it, and we still have bags full of stuff that never made it onto the scrapbook pages.

The process of committing my adult reflections to paper/PC now has involved a challenge to shift my head from thinking of this as some random, personal recollections – and extended diary – to it being something that might actually be read by other people. There's a confidence required by this process which hasn't come naturally, even though I've written as part of my work for years. This is about me, my children, and our lives – and by my nature, I'm not given to great outpourings of personal stories.

Ultimately, though I felt that, this year, I needed to write these things down. Committing my feelings completely honestly to paper in the first years after Jon died was cathartic at the time. I know, reading my words now, that the rawness and pain, but also the joy and occasional celebration of our life then as three, were authentic. Fifteen years on, I felt that the rest of the story, to date, also needed to be out of me, and not left bubbling around inside. Writing things down has forced me to tie up the loose ends of any emotional issue that had been left hanging. It has encouraged me to try and make sense or draw conclusions; to draw a line under events and to make peace with them. I said in Chapter 1 that the idea of gaining 'closure' or moving on after Jon's funeral was beyond my grasp. I'm still not convinced that there can ever be closure after any loss, let alone by suicide; but I do find from my own experience, writing my story — initially in my diary — and now here, has been helpful in moving me further down the path towards whatever has come, and will come, next.

SOME THINGS JON DIDN'T KNOW ABOUT

9/11 and the war on terror

Social media

All the friends we've met since the children went to nursery (my entire, local social network)

The omnipresence of herbal tea

The rise of quinoa

Smartphones and my inability to use them (he wouldn't have been surprised)

I am vaguely competent on a word processor (he would have been surprised)

All our friends' children who have been born since he died

Cheap flights around the world

A Scottish Wimbledon and Olympic tennis champion

His dad died

A black president of the USA

Brexit

Trump

CHAPTER 3

FALLING OFF THE CONVEYOR BELT

Our family stopped evolving in the regular way the instant Jon died. Everybody else kept moving along, living their lives on a fairly steady path, moving through life's ups and downs in a reasonably predictable, two-partnered way. Everything about a life like that was blown out of the water for us. For a long time I felt it as a visceral, physical pain, because there were just too many in-our-face reminders of what we had lost. The bittersweet times spent with friends we loved were also the starkest indicators of how off-kilter our lives were in comparison.

We can never catch up with that conveyor belt which kept going without us. But the pain it used to provoke is much less. Being the three of us became our everyday experience a very long time ago, and by 2010 I had lived more of my life without Jon than I had shared with him. We got onto our own parallel conveyor belt, on which Eilidh and Cameron have never known what it's really like to grow up in a family with two parents. Their ordinary is the three of us. They have spent weekend or holiday time with families who have two parents, but that's not the same as living everyday life in the family dynamics that come with having two adults here. I sometimes wonder how they will cope with family life if and when they meet their own partners in future, and whether they will find it odd to be in a household where there are two grown-ups all the time.

My emotional benchmark is now our family of three, and for years that has felt OK. But life's conveyor belt still catches me unawares. Nowadays, the big life event in our group of friends is children heading off, making plans to go to university, or out into the world in some other way. For all our friends, the brief ache at the loss of their offspring is more than matched by the 'yippee!' of making plans for their newly re-found freedom to have adventures as a couple. I'm making my own plans. But by necessity, they will be different to everyone else's. And I now see that the world is full of all sorts of different conveyor belts, running alongside, round about, or up and over each other. The trick is finding the right one to climb aboard.

SCREAMING INSIDE MY HEAD

Warning: Rant ahead. If you think you might not want to hear it, feel free to skip the next paragraphs. But for anyone who really wants to get inside the head of an occasionally enraged bereaved woman, read on.

Screaming inside my head never happened before Jon died. I don't think I'd ever felt real anger until then. I got upset, I felt aggrieved, I felt sad. But anger was not an emotion with which I was familiar. Boy, have I felt it in huge, and sometimes irrational spadesful since then.

I say elsewhere in this story that I never felt angry with Jon. And I really didn't. But I have felt ragingly angry with the situation we found ourselves in, with the stupidity of the things people have said, and the things that my children have had to put up with in their lives without their dad. Anger isn't a rational thing, and it feels scary and at times overwhelming. But it is a response to provocations, and if it can be subdued and addressed healthily, it can hopefully help to make sense of those provocations, and resolve the underlying issue.

The early screaming in my head was all about the unbelievableness of finding myself widowed at the age of 35, having two small children, and being out in the world, looking passably sane, but feeling far from it. The tension between my internal screaming and the external apparent normality just made the insanity of it all even worse.

As the years have passed, my screaming has had more to do with the things people say or do – and people say crass things.

Not out of badness, not even really thoughtlessness. Heck, even the most sensitive, emotionally intelligent people occasionally let slip a thoughtless thing, because their mouth engages before their brain, or it's the end of a long day. Whatever; I know I've done it on occasion, and felt very bad afterwards. So I don't judge what people have said to me over the years, although at the time I could very easily have let them know how it made me feel – but I never have done. I've bitten my lip, nodded, or maybe made a sympathetic sound. Because what they don't want to hear is the tirade that plays out in my head – 'No, I'm sorry, but my husband taking his own life and never coming back is not the same as your husband working away from home one or two nights a week. It's not the same as being divorced, when you can have every other weekend to yourself. It's not the same as occasionally having to go to a party by yourself because your husband's feeling anti-social'.

Maybe I should have dipped my toe in the water of social honesty. But I knew, even as people said those things, they had no idea of the impact they were having, and would, I suspect, have felt terrible if they knew how bereft and lonely they made me feel. Really walking in someone else's shoes – genuinely empathising – is very rare. And it's unrealistic to expect someone who hasn't experienced this to be able to inhabit the depths of what it feels like. And I wouldn't wish it on anyone. There are endless terrible, traumatic situations that people suffer, survive or struggle through every day. I can imagine some of them, and I can intellectually or emotionally feel for those people – but I am not living their lives, and I would not presume to fully understand what that means.

I'm not comparing my life experience with others', or trying to place it on some kind of scale of bad things that happen. It is, simply, my experience, and in sharing it, all I hope is that it may have some resonance if you've been through something similar. Perhaps you'll realise, as a result, that you're not the only one. And as for the things friends and others may say, be grateful for the ones who get it, and try to let go of your anger with the ones who don't.

Is my protective maternal instinct stronger than other parents' who haven't lost a partner? I don't know, because this is the only way of parenting two children I've ever known. But I do know that there have been times when other people – mostly children, but not always – have said things which have hurt Eilidh or Cameron. I was not proud of how angry I felt, or what I felt capable of doing to those people. More than anything, I was furious at their lack of imagination, furious that my children – on top of just dealing with being kids in the twenty-first century – have to live every day as the children of a dad who took his own life.

To this day, all my mama-bear instincts get fired up when someone does or says something hurtful or wounding to the children, even if it has nothing to do with their dad. And I know that behind my reaction is still this sense of unfairness about how much more they have had to deal with than most children.

Rant over.

CAM'S PASSIONS (IN ORDER, FROM TODDLERHOOD)...ALL BOY

Diggers	Lego
Tractors	Warhammer
Herbie (the VW)	Iron Man
Transformers	...and I learnt to draw all of
Lightning McQueen	them except the last two.
Transformers again	He was a hard taskmaster.

CHAPTER 4

THE NOT-RULES OF GRIEF AND MOURNING

There are some well-known theories of what happens during grief (the automatic, emotional, physical, gut reaction to a bereavement) and mourning (the much longer, for some never-ending, process of working through the loss, and hopefully, eventually, finding some way of living comfortably with it).

I studied some of these when I was training to be a social worker, so the structure of them has been in my head for a long time. With hindsight, and occasional objectivity, living through my own loss was a salutary experience in the context of 'theories'. I finally felt and understood what all the theorists and commentators always noted as their proviso – that no theory can explain everything about your own grief and loss, that there are no right ways of mourning, nor any right order to the stages that are posited. In the examples that follow, Elisabeth Kübler-Ross refers to five stages, Mardi Horowitz to four and Therese Rando to six.

I have felt and experienced all of their stages, and variations of them, throughout the past 15 years. I've revisited most of them multiple times, bounced through some more quickly than others, lingered painfully in some, and certainly didn't work through them in any kind of neat, pre-planned order. The value of them, I've come to recognise, is that having a basic grasp of the theories does help to remind you that you're going along a real and much travelled path, that anyone who has been bereaved has felt most of the things you've felt, and that, on the days when you feel as if you're losing your mind, there's an explanation for why you feel like that. And, reassuringly, no matter how long your mourning lasts, and how painful and relentless it might sometimes feel, you understand that there will be, for most people, a time when you realise you feel better. Indefinably, and unpredictably, but definitely better.

So, in no way an expert view, but in an everyday nutshell, the following few pages are the essence of what's going on at different points along the grief and mourning paths. These are not rules about how it should be done. There is no right or wrong way, only the way that works for you to get through it. These are experiences you may recognise. Not a tick list to be checked off, but maybe a slightly comforting sense of recognising a phase that you've been through, and may not have to go through again. But if you do, know that you're not alone in it.

FIVE-STAGE THEORY

Elisabeth Kübler-Ross developed a five-stage theory in the 1950s, which has been the foundation on which others have built. The stages she used were Denial, Anger, Bargaining, Depression and Acceptance.

Denial is what happens in the first shocked days after a loss, when everything feels unreal, and the overriding sense is of being desperate to wake from a bad dream.

Anger comes with the realisation that the loss is real, when you might rage against the world and the unfairness of what has happened. There can be feelings of abandonment and anger against the person for leaving, or against other people who might be deemed 'responsible' for their death.

Bargaining is about trying to reverse the loss, when the desperate longing for the person means feeling you'd do anything to have them back – like making deals with God, or whoever will listen, that you'll be a better person if only they could still be here.

Depression comes with the realisation that those bargaining deals are not going to happen. This confrontation with reality can lead to a time of deep sadness, crying and openly grieving. It can be a time of withdrawing from those closest to you, and from the world in general. Sleeping and eating habits can change, doing more or less of either. For some, it is a time of self-blame, questioning what you could have done to stop your loved one dying. This is very strongly felt in those who have lost someone through suicide.

Acceptance comes when you find yourself able to look ahead instead of only backwards, and to re-engage with your life.

FOUR-STAGE THEORY

The pattern above is described slightly differently by Mardi Horowitz. I like his language (1990s instead of 1950s), and his stages make sense to me: Outcry, Denial and intrusion, Working through, and Completion.

Outcry can literally be that – a verbal outpouring of grief when the loved person dies, screaming, crying or physically collapsing. It is the absolute, unbidden, natural reaction to the devastating news of your loss. For other people, their instinctive reaction is to hold the distress inside, an invisible manifestation of shock and grief, but no less intense for its internality. The energy needed to sustain emotions at either of these pitches – overt and external, or held in and overwhelmed – is huge, and can't be maintained for long.

Denial and intrusion are what tend to follow – for days, weeks or years. They are the extremes of wanting to keep endlessly busy and occupied to distract from the pain of grief, set against the sense of being overwhelmed by its intrusion, and wanting to withdraw from life. Often the denial is conscious. It was for me, and I knew that for as long as I kept cramming our days full of activity and tasks and being involved in things, it was putting off the inevitable emotional crash. And from the outset, I knew there would be a time when the children would be old enough not to need me every minute of every day, and would be resilient enough. It wasn't a thought-through decision, but I knew in my head that by then it would be OK to let the crash happen. Until that time, I rationed my moments of intrusion to the times when I could be alone. Early on, I was driving back (probably too fast, listening to some over-emotive Coldplay) by myself from a friend's 40th birthday in the Highlands, down a beautiful road near the west coast. It was a road that Jon had known well, surrounded by the mountains he had loved being in and at the top of, and I raged and cried at the unfairness and injustice that he'd never do that with his children, or show them his favourite high places. By the time I reached Fort William, I'd cried myself out. Those alone-times were few and far between, but they were a slight safety valve against the held-in, kept-together, crazy-busy stuff that went on the rest of the time. Horowitz pointed out that the Denial (not denying the loss, but being distracted from it) is not a bad thing. It allows some kind of respite for those for whom the intrusion of emotions is more overwhelming in the early stages, a breathing space which comes through being busy, and allows the intrusions of grief to be handled in smaller doses. For some people, the swinging between the two extremes of Intrusion and Denial can be unexpected and frequent; for others, less so.

Working through follows when the distraction from loss becomes more commonplace and less frenetic than its painful intrusions. This is the start of being able to look ahead and contemplate that there might be a way of living positively in the future without the person you loved.

Completion of mourning (or 'completed enough' to allow life to start feeling like a new version of ordinary) comes next, when the pain of loss feels less acute.

Remember that in all of these stages, and those of the other theorists, there is no fixed timescale. Some people experience mourning over a period of months, some over years. Although the stages are listed in order, there is no fixed 'routine' to how you get through them. When you've been back to denial and intrusion, or anger, or depression for the umpteenth time, and you have the voice screaming inside your head that you are *never* going to be at acceptance or completion because it is all so raw and ugly and painful, and you don't want to be anyway because you're still holding onto the hope that your most loved person hasn't actually died...just believe that you *can* get to a happier and safer-feeling place.

It may take a long time. Things will never feel like they did before. But life can feel good again. You may not be able to contemplate it just now, but you will be able to feel happy without feeling guilty about it. You'll be able to take joy from things here and now, and to think of the person you've lost with warmth and happiness for the life and experiences you shared, and not only for the space they've left in your life and your being. Above all, you will be able to do all of this without feeling disloyal to them.

THE SIX RS

Therese Rando has developed her theories of grieving and mourning since the 1970s. Her 'Six Rs' are a list of 'instructions' for the bereaved person. Even if they don't happen in the order she writes them, like all the stages outlined by the other theorists, each is a crucial part of being able to eventually reach the 'completed enough' stage. An unresolved grief, where one or more stages aren't passed through at some point, will remain unresolved. It may sit very deeply buried inside, and the world will see someone who to all extents and purposes is getting on with their life and coping brilliantly.

But a volcano with a lid on top is likely to erupt explosively if it doesn't have small eruptions to act as safety valves along the way.

Recognise your loss. Experience it and understand that it has happened. This is particularly difficult with deaths by suicide or murder, and may not happen for some time afterwards.

React emotionally to your loss. The reality is that when your partner has died, your loss is not just of that person and your relationship with them, but also your role as their partner, your plans for your shared future, and maybe a loss of faith in humanity, or in your god or other beliefs. The enormity of this cannot be processed in a short time. Everything you took for granted has been uprooted, and you need to be gentle with yourself as you allow yourself to mourn all of these separate bits of your life, and this can catch you unawares at the most unexpected times.

I was having coffee in the upstairs coffee shop at our local bookshop, a year or so after Jon died. Looking down on all the bookshelves and display tables, I felt an upsurge of sadness that Jon wouldn't have the chance to read all those books and soak up all that knowledge, or share it with the children. He *loved* reading; loved nothing more than a Saturday morning at a second-hand bookshop or sale, and coming home with armfuls of weird books about windsurfing, plank-on-frame model-boat building, or Chaos theory. He bought books he thought the children would like before we even had children. I love reading, too, but looking at that bookstore, I knew I'd never be able to convey the massive enthusiasm and energy for absorbing facts and ideas about a crazy range of things which he had. In that moment, I felt the books represented all the things Jon could have shared with Eilidh and Cameron, which they'd miss out on now. I'd always had him down as the parent who'd do the clever, informative (scientific) stuff and teach them how to ski, or grow bonsai trees, or do bike repairs. (He made me read a book about bike repairs once. I'm still not interested enough to do it myself…)

As it's turned out, neither of our children seems particularly interested in small trees yet. But they both ski, having never read a book about it. Cameron has inherited his dad's scientific genes and absorbs facts like a sponge, and Eilidh his spirit of adventure.

So many parts of Jon are in both of the children, they've instinctively channelled all the bits of him we'd have encouraged had he still been with us, and I've just tried to support and encourage them along the way.

The moral of this brief diversion is that that yes, you need to react to your loss, in whatever guise it appears, and at whatever different times. But keep in mind that while your life won't be the same again, nor what you imagined it would be, it can be something different and brilliant all the same.

Recollecting and re-experiencing are important next, says Rando. This is about honestly remembering the good and less good parts of your life and relationship together so that you form a truthful picture of your partner to carry forward with you. In some ways this may be when 'laying someone to rest' can properly happen. In all relationships I suspect there will have been elements that are less happy to recall. The instinct to remember only the best, most joyful memories is understandable and automatic. Letting yourself acknowledge the harder parts of a relationship is more difficult. It feels disloyal. It feels as if you may slip into a spiral of negative memories. Especially if you're trying to form a version of your partner to share with your children, to be the memory they have throughout their lives, it's natural to try and expurgate the more painful memories.

In my experience, this was only ever a barrier to being able to keep moving through mourning. Jon was an exciting and wonderful partner in many ways (see lists elsewhere). But he was often difficult to live with, and made me feel bad about myself. With hindsight, I suspect a lot of this was connected with whatever aspect of his mental health ultimately led him to take his own life. I know he loved me and the children without reservation. But he was still difficult to live with.

I have only been able to acknowledge different aspects of this piecemeal, and over a period of many years. But with each honest acknowledgement, I've felt a sense of relief and peace, as if that negative memory can now be packed away and not revisited, whereas if it remained unacknowledged, it would still be waiting to be dealt with.

Relinquishing old attachments can begin next. This isn't about abandoning your partner's memory: In recollecting and re-experiencing, you were hopefully able to put memories in a safe and comfortable place. Relinquishing is more about giving yourself permission to start to put your loss behind you, and accept that the world has permanently changed. As with Horowitz's 'working through' it may take some time to get to this point. And it can feel scary and as if you want to resist it, because after your initial grief, letting go of the past will be one of the hardest things you've done. But it is possible.

Readjusting follows, hopefully, when your loss will feel less acute, and you can contemplate the reality of returning to everyday life, or at least a new everyday.

Re-investment comes next, a process which is akin to completion or acceptance. You'll realise you feel like or already have created space for new things in your life, while maintaining space for the partner you lost. You'll be able to make new attachments and commitments, accept these changes, and be happy about them.

As I said at the start of this chapter, these are not rules. Working through mourning – which feels nothing like productive, everyday 'work' – is exhausting, and being told that there are theories to help explain what it's all about can make you want to throw things at the wall. What all of these stages and theories *can* offer is the reassurance that, for almost everyone, the rawness of grief will lessen over time, and while you might not recognise each diminution of pain as it happens, in later years it will be possible to look back and know that things are much, much better than they were.

POSSIBLE EFFECTS OF BEREAVEMENT

Feeling exhausted (to your bones)

Full of energy and totally alert

Difficulty sleeping

Difficulty staying awake

Eating more

Eating less

Muscle tremors

Chills

Sweats

Temporary hearing loss or vision impairment

Difficulty breathing

Rapid breathing

Increased heart rate or blood pressure

Breast milk dries up (nursing mothers)

Stomach problems

Nausea/dizziness

Confusion (problems with memory, concentration, judgement or comprehension)

Intrusion of unwanted thoughts or bad dreams

Dissociation (detachment, disorientation, denial)

Shock

Fear

Anxiety, agitation

Numbness, remoteness, depression

Anger, irritability

Guilt

LOOKING AFTER YOURSELF

All of the symptoms listed above are possible; some are probable. Hopefully, usually, they don't all happen at once. If you feel any of these signs are overwhelming, please ask for help and support from someone you trust. If you prefer a DIY approach, I found the following helpful at different times.

Eat and sleep as well as you can. It's very easy to neglect these, and good sleep may be hard to come by. If you have children who keep antisocial bedtime hours, this will be even more likely. When Eilidh and Cameron were little, I napped when they napped, even if it was for ten minutes when we arrived somewhere after driving. Eating well might be easier with children because you have to feed them. The temptation when you're by yourself might be to live on a packet of biscuits. Remember to feed yourself, too.

Keep in touch with friends and family and be as sociable as you can. On some days you may feel like bolting the door and avoiding the world. That's OK on some days, but not on all of them. It takes a great effort of will to get dressed up, stick on a brave face and go and play, but it will reconnect you with your other self. And it gets easier.

Put off making big decisions for a while, moving house or changing job, for example. Your inclination might be to change things dramatically to try and distract from your grief, to escape painful memories or perhaps to move closer to people who care about you. If you allow yourself some time to work out what you really feel about these things, your decision is likely to be a clearer and better informed one. My own experience was that staying put, in the same house, in the same job, provided safety and security for all of us. I did change jobs, but only a sideways move, and stayed in touch with my old work friends. We still live in the house Jon and I bought before we got married. Over the past 15 years, we've had work done, and redecorated more than once, so it doesn't look exactly like the same place, and I did feel guilty when I made the first changes, thinking it was disloyal to Jon somehow. But it wasn't – he and I would have redecorated by then anyway. (Who has deep red dining room walls these days?)

Your loved one's belongings. There's no right or wrong thing to do with these. I know some people keep things forever, or for years before they feel able to let them out of the house. I've done a mixture. I got rid of Jon's work suits almost immediately. They didn't represent who he was for me or the children, and in fact I felt they were connected to all the more negative connotations of his work. Within weeks, I found a charity which supported men trying to get back into work, and took them all there.

I did keep specific pieces of clothing which Jon had either been wearing in photos with the children, or which were so powerfully evocative of him I couldn't let them go – his rugby shirts, the baggy old cream sweater his mum knitted when he was a student and I'd known him wear since I first knew him, the faded old shirts he never threw away and wore constantly, the ancient boxer shorts which had long since lost their elastic and were so faded I couldn't work out what the pattern was. They are all in boxes in the attic. I was about to write that I'm not sentimental, and that the children can choose what to do with them – Eilidh has long worn his T-shirts as pyjamas – but contemplating that, I realise that his clothes most strongly bring back memories of him, and so I'll probably leave them there for a while longer. Cameron tried on Jon's kilt for the first time a few weeks ago. It fitted perfectly, and made me cry.

I've mentioned Jon's books more than once. I've had to be pragmatic. Our own collections over the last 15 years would never have fitted if I'd kept everything that had been his. So at different times, I've had various book culls, some more radical than others. But I've kept what I thought was a good representation of his loves and enthusiasms. And the children know that the world to which you can escape in books, or the learning to be gained from them, was held very dear by their dad, and they have inherited that from him.

Do some exercise – whatever you enjoy. It's good for your body, but good for your head and your spirit too. It's not about losing weight or getting in great shape, but more about carving out some time for you. And working out hard in the gym, listening to loud music on the iPod, or climbing a hill can be good therapy.

Do the things that make you feel good. My feel-good things have always been gardening, being outside, walking and cycling: breathing clean air, being aware of the world around me. And I love making things – jewellery, patchwork, stained glass. And eating and drinking. All of these are 100 per cent better done with friends. Remember the things you love, and try and do them as often as is possible. If you have young children, you need to be creative about how and when you can fit them in, but even if that is briefly, once a week (and for a while that may be all that's possible), guard those times closely. And work out the things to which you can bring the children along for the ride.

Cut yourself some slack. Be kind to yourself, and shift your expectations. You don't have to get everything done *today*, or even tomorrow.

A WORD ABOUT STIGMA AND SHAME

The dynamics of grieving for someone who took their own life are different to coping with the loss of someone through illness, old age, accident or murder. They are all painful and difficult processes. And the 'not-rules' outlined earlier in this chapter apply to all the situations in varying degrees. But suicide, despite the times we live in, has – for some people – the added load of stigma and shame.

Even before Jon died, I had never regarded suicide as something to be ashamed of or whispered about or hidden from public view, although I was aware that some people did. My mum's youngest sister took her own life when I was 15, and had spent years struggling to control the anorexia which was the outward symptom of her fragile mental health. From the age of 10, when she made the first attempt on her life, I understood that such a choice was possible, and grew up feeling compassion for her, or anyone else who felt so desperate that ending their life was the only solution to their problems. I absolutely believed, contrary to the idea that suicide is an act of cowardice, that in fact it took incredible courage – although it was the act of someone so removed from reality or rational thought that it could not be compared with more conventional definitions of 'courage'. This in no way diminished the emotionally devastating impact Jon's death had on me and the children, and after he died, I felt the pain of any bereavement – huge sadness for him, and a longing that he could have let me help him better. But I had no sense of shame or stigma.

And, for the most part, I have only encountered similarly compassionate views from friends and my family in the years since he died. But I am aware that there are others who find the issue of suicide shameful and stigmatising. Many people still talk about someone 'committing' suicide, which instantly criminalises the act, although it was decriminalised in England in 1961 and was never illegal in Scotland. 'Self-murder' had been a mortal sin in the eyes of the Church long before it was criminalised by law in the thirteenth century. People who made failed attempts on their own life were often prosecuted and imprisoned, even until the 1950s, and if they succeeded in taking their own life, their families could be punished and (in the past) often had to forfeit their possessions to the Crown. It is hard to imagine the mindset of the churchmen and lawmakers who thought that the most effective way to deal with someone so desperate as to end their own life was to imprison them and socially stigmatise their family.

The Church was considerably ahead of the law when it allowed the burial of suicide victims in consecrated ground in 1823; although they were only allowed a religious ceremony 50 years later (and even then, not the official Burial Service). It took 80 years for Parliament to catch up and pass the Suicide Act in 1961, finally displaying much needed compassion and empathy for the victims of suicide and their families. But despite those various religious and secular changes in law, stretching back over nearly 200 years, there remains a niggling belief for some people that there is something 'sinful' or shameful about suicide, and that it shouldn't be spoken about. It is a terrible tragedy, yes. It devastates the lives of the people left behind, yes. It often leaves a trail of unanswered questions, yes. But it *has* to be talked about – to keep the more brilliant memories of the loved one alive, but also to allow an honest understanding of mental health pain, so we can try and prevent it happening to other people. Remembering Jon with love, compassion and joy for all the fantastic bits of his life is a much better legacy than feeling ashamed of the brief act that ended his life.

CHAPTER 5

AND THE WALLS CAME TUMBLING DOWN

I knew they would at some point. It was only a matter of time. I always wondered what the trigger would be, and suspected that the children being old enough for me not to worry too much about them might have something to do with it. Not that I planned it. I might have been holding on tightly to control in my life, but this one was beyond me.

It happened in the autumn of 2009. I had gone on for eight years, trying to be the best possible parent. Being responsible for all of us, and keeping our homely ship afloat, loving and laughing with the children, working, having time with friends. As time wore on though, the effort of being the only protective parent became increasingly exhausting. Everything I did was about keeping the children feeling physically and emotionally safe and secure. I could just about keep up with what was needed to make that happen inside our four walls, although it sometimes took what felt like superhuman resolve and willpower. What I couldn't control were things that went on outside and round about us.

About the time that Jon died, the old man who had lived in the house adjoining ours walked out one day to go and live with his sister on the other side of town, and he never came back. His house was already in a fair state of disrepair, but after that it quickly became much worse. The roof was badly in need of patching (replacing, as it turned out, many years later), and the front and back gardens were so overgrown it was impossible to see what was hidden under the rambling creepers and weeds. It soon became a target for kids roaming past, and windows were broken and more rubbish piled into the gardens. Over the years, because we were so closely adjoined, our house got targeted too, and we had beer bottles thrown through the windows at night, and other less identifiable missiles too (although the Pot Noodle was quite obvious).

We live in a quiet, pleasant area, but for years, on top of the issue of the abandoned house next door, the road past our house was the route of choice for all late-night revellers heading home in the wee small hours, some fairly peaceable but others loud and aggressive, swearing and singing. For a while, the crossroads outside seemed to be the gathering point for big crowds of the noisy, swearing, shouting ones, and I would lie in bed willing them to keep walking, and to not have anything in their hands that might end up being pitched through my window. I dreaded the weekends, when it always seemed to be busier and noisier; but as time passed, weekday nights were not immune either. I woke at the slightest noise, and lay wide awake listening for any tell-tale signs that someone might be about to throw something, or worse, break into our house. My over-riding fear was that something would happen to the children, and I was overwhelmed by my need to protect them. But I was also scared, and angry at the thoughtless, faceless idiots who made me feel that way.

The tipping point came gradually as 2009 went by. The cumulative impact of all the disturbed nights and anxiety that went with them continued to mount. A close friend in America died in the spring. Finally, after anticipating it for years, one night some kids broke into the house next door at three o'clock in the morning and started smashing the internal doors down. It sounded as if they were in our house, and even when we worked out that they weren't, we were still shaken and terrified (and trying to be cheery and reassuring for the children took more resolve than I knew I had). The final straw was receiving a handful of anonymous and threatening sexual phone calls. I have no idea who made them, but they were enough to shatter the final vestiges of any courage I'd had until that point.

I fell apart. I was exhausted from carrying the fear of some unknown threat to the children, and the weight of responsibility for everything else over the past eight years. I felt emotionally assaulted by unknown people, and so incredibly alone in trying to deal with it all. And because all I'd been trying to do was be as good a person as possible, it was beyond my comprehension that those people could punish me so powerfully. Of course, that was the product of my exhausted mind and soul, and my inability to think rationally any more. I'm sure none of what happened was directed at us personally, but after so many years of holding everything together, it all felt like part of the same parcel of bad things I couldn't handle any more.

My wonderful Dad came and stayed with us for a few days, and my friend Abigail was the other half of my scaffolding for that weird, disorientating time. I went to the GP, and told him the whole story of Jon's death and more recent events, and how important it was for me to polish the children's shoes every week (the surest sign of a loss of perspective). And after he said, 'Shit, that's terrible' (I'd always thought of him as a very proper person) he prescribed some low-level anti-anxiety pills, and made a referral for some Cognitive Behavioural Therapy (CBT) sessions. Bizarrely, I went for a job interview in the middle of those few crazy days, and got the job. My recollection is that I was bouncing off the walls and observing the whole process from the ceiling in equal measure, but my boss assures me I seemed fine (and employable).

I had the CBT sessions, and I also went to a Mindfulness course for a few months (for details see the Appendix). We made a few practical changes in the house so I felt less vulnerable. Between all of that and a brief spell taking the tablets, I was able to remember how to feel calm and safe and that I was doing an OK job. And Mum and Dad, as ever, mopped up the overspill, and I think the children were blissfully ignorant of what was really going on for the worst of it.

I was lucky that I could regain some kind of equilibrium relatively quickly. I would never want to live through a time like that again, but having survived it, it made my return to the real world much sweeter. I had known that there would probably need to be some great outpouring of grief and rage and fear and sadness after Jon's death. I had no idea how long afterwards it would come, and I had built some fairly serious defences to ensure it didn't happen too quickly. From the vantage point of 15 years, I look back at that time, and another lesser one much more recently, and wonder if there is a 'healthier' way of grieving. Maybe those cultures where overt and painful grief, public wailing and expression of loss are the norm? Or allowing oneself to crack at regular intervals so that hopefully the pain is released and the safety valve engaged so there are no mammoth blow-outs? Possibly. But as the previous chapter showed, there really are no right or wrong ways of getting through grief. This is the way I've done it; not *chosen* to do it, but just instinctively started on one path, and kept following it to where it is (and I am) now.

CHAPTER 6

'TOO STIFF A TREE TO BEAR THE WEIGHT'[1]

WHY MEN?

In 2017, 6639 people took their own life in the UK and Republic of Ireland. Three-quarters of them were men. The rates per 100,000 and gender proportions differ slightly between Scotland, England, Wales and Ireland. But the trend over a period of many years has been basically the same. Three times more men kill themselves than women each year. In the UK the highest suicide rate for men is in the 40–44 year age group. In the Republic of Ireland it is highest in those aged 25–34 years, and it is almost identical for those aged between 45 and 54.[2]

When I made contact with the bereaved children's charity Winston's Wish in 2007, it was to seek support for the children. It didn't occur to me that it might help me too. When the children gathered for their residential weekend, the parents and carers were invited to take part in their own weekend group. Not having anything else to do in Gloucestershire for two days, I signed up;

---

1   This chapter title is taken from *Ruby* by Cynthia Bond (2015), who referred to the idea that someone could hold themselves so emotionally taut and rigid, that they appeared strong and defended – but would then be broken by a strong wind or load.
2   See https://www.samaritans.org/about-us/our-research/facts-and-figures-about-suicide.

I really hadn't thought I needed it. But I've been grateful ever since that I went. Not just because the group leaders were so insightful, skilled and supportive, and nurtured and cared for us so well, but because we made friendships which have lasted. No one who hasn't experienced it knows what it's like to lose a partner to suicide, and although we rarely talk about it explicitly when we get together, we know we have an understanding of that shared similarity in our histories.

Lots of aspects of that weekend have stayed with me, but one in particular has never lost its impact. The first exercise we did together as a group on the first morning was to create a chart – half-a-wall-sized, huge – of who we had lost, how old they were when they died, and how they died. There were ten of us in the group. We were all women. And the ones who took their own lives were our male partners or husbands. And all fathers. Ten men: their names and end-of-life stories written in bold, on the wall for the duration of our weekend together.

That still takes my breath away. It was shocking, and desperately sad. All the men were around the same age as Jon when they died. Since losing Jon I had often thought about what drives men, especially relatively young men, to take their own lives – but here was a stark and brutally clear image of ten fathers – partners – who had made that decision. Who had decided, no matter how irrational it may have seemed to others, that their only option was to leave their families forever, believing that by doing so they would be taking their pain out of the family equation, and thereby 'sparing' them. But, in fact, leaving them devastated and bereft.

In the first few years after Jon died I worked on a book in my head, and occasionally on paper. I think it was part of my strategy to help me get through that time. It was about men, the way they live their lives, the pressures they face, whether these were different to those faced by women, and about trying to make sense of Jon's death. As I said in the Introduction, I then read *Manhood* by Steve Biddulph, and discovered he'd already written 'my' book, the general male aspects anyway. But living with thoughts of Jon for 15 years, and of the other men who made the same choice to end their lives as he did, my ideas about why that might be have crystallised. For all our societal efforts to seek parity between the genders, men and women really aren't the same. I'm not going to have a discussion about feminism or gender equality, because what follows here is about men and the ways they differ from women, which make the experience of being in this world intolerable for some of them. And statistically, it is very clear that this experience, or the response to it, is not the same for women as it is for men.

At its most simplistic, some of this is about men feeling unclear about what it actually means today to be 'manly'. In the past (and the not too distant past in some parts of the UK) it was very easy to demonstrate manliness. Jobs were physically hard and demanding – mining, farming, heavy industry. They involved long hours working in tough physical conditions, where, by dint of the work they did, men expressed their physical strength, and their ability to survive in that hard and uncompromising world. The political, economic and social changes in the UK over the past 30 years have forcibly changed the landscape of the male world of work. The heartlands of British heavy industry have been shut down, and their working populations left either jobless or re-employed in service, financial or light industries. There had always been men working in those fields, but now there was no choice. In many communities where the industrial heart was destroyed, nothing was put in to replace it. The purpose of many men's lives was lost.

Physical exercise has always been an outlet for men's (and women's) energy and emotions, although in the past, when work was physically demanding in itself, the need for this was less. Today, I don't think the waves of marathon runners, mountain bikers and extreme sportsmen are all just in it for the physical and mental health benefits. I think it meets a physical need that is unmet in daily working, or unemployed, life. It demonstrates the physical strength and commitment that can't be proved by a man who is jobless or at an office desk. In his recent TV series 'All Man', Grayson Perry met cage fighters in the North East of England. The mining and industrial jobs which previous generations of men did don't exist any more. For young men in those communities, fighting is an outward demonstration of their maleness. It's the same kind of outlet as the boxing clubs which have channelled young boy's and men's energies in inner cities for years.

The sensitivity and insightfulness of the men involved in that TV programme were striking. All had experienced physical or emotional hardship in their earlier lives, and were remarkably articulate about this. But they admitted that it would have been impossible for them to be so without the outward badge of maleness they earned by cage fighting.

Because, of course, in our society showing emotions is not 'manly'. How old are boys when they learn they shouldn't cry? There's a scene in the film *Big* when Tom Hanks's character, who has been magically turned into an adult but is actually only 12 years old, finds himself alone in a seedy hotel in New York. The boy is scared and lonely, and he lies on a filthy bed and cries; but what we see is the adult face of the child inside crying. And grown-up men aren't meant to cry. It always struck me that being alone in a big city, in a divey hotel, would never feel great, but there comes a time when you learn that you just can't cry about stuff like that. And that's what gives the scene its power.

EMOTIONAL OPENNESS

Even for the men I've grown up with (who are the ones I know best), emotional openness and talking about feelings can be a daunting arena – and the men I know are open-minded, intelligent, sociable people. I don't think many would refute the fact that they were raised in families where there wasn't a lot of emotional chit chat, or wearing-your-heart-on-your-sleeve kind of conversations. Discussing the way they felt about events in their lives wasn't often encouraged or supported. At one level I get this: deep and meaningfuls about relationships or 'mushy' stuff aren't the natural territory of the male conversationalist. I know that many male friends' default settings for chat are wide-ranging – shared sporting loves or exercise and activity plans, music, politics, scientific issues, holidays, curry recipes, work and the state of the world. My women friends of the same age talk about all of those things. But also about our children, our relationships and friendships, and what we *feel* about all of the above. Granted, I can think of some exceptions to these rules, but I hope the generalisation makes its point. Men and women communicate differently, and they have different needs from their relationships with other people.

To be fair, though, my experience is that despite their upbringing in environments where emotional openness, especially with their fathers, wasn't usual, most of these men have forged close and expressive relationships with their own children. They have built these relationships around shared adventures and experiences, and being actively involved in all aspects of their lives. They know them and understand them in ways which I don't think many of their fathers knew or understood them. And it is vital for boys to have this kind of relationship with their dads. Or, for boys without fathers, with close male family friends or relatives who can mentor them in the ways of growing up into the adult male world.

In general, boys and men, by their natures, or in the way that some are raised or nutured, don't relate to each other in the same openly emotional ways as girls and women, but tend to build closeness based on shared experiences. And in their daily lives, working and social, the need for pragmatism and clarity of thought usually takes precedence over a more emotive approach. But, alongside all the other aspects of being in the world of men, it needs to be OK for them to acknowledge and share their emotional responses to life and events, and to have these responses supported and validated by those closest to them. As the mother of a son, I think this is crucially important.

SOCIAL PRESSURES

On this path to men's emotional self-discovery the idea of the New Man arose in the 1980s as one response to the feminist movement. Historically – and admittedly this is generalising and doing a disservice to those families who were ahead of the trend – clearly defined and distinct gender roles had allowed a simple division of domestic roles. Fathers were usually the full time bread-winners, DIY or mechanical experts, and briefly involved parents at the evening or at weekends. Mothers were the primary care-givers throughout a child's life, and responsible for everyday domestic chores and tasks. New Men suddenly had to be sensitive to their partner's feelings, voluntarily wash the dishes, change the baby's nappies, be a 'hands-on' dad, and definitely not be like their fathers had been. There were a lot of positives in this, not least that today, hands-on dads are no longer unusual or even newsworthy, and the benefits to children and fathers are manifest. And domestic bliss may not always be blissful, but is certainly more egalitarian for many couples and families.

New Lads appeared as a counter-reaction in the 1990s – hard-working (sometimes), hard-playing (often), irresponsible and edgy. Later came the Metrosexuals – more like the New Men, but trendier. And today, they have morphed into the Hipsters – like New Men and Metrosexuals, but with beards.

And what lies between the lines of all of these evolutionary stages is that the past 30 years have placed huge expectations on the shoulders of men to become something additional to, or better than, or different to what they were before – which in traditional terms was actually quite simple. Breadwinner, head of the household, 'strong silent type', not mother. Now, 'being a good dad' (for which, read 'involved') for men with children has become an essential requisite of family life. This isn't a bad thing: men and their partners and children will all benefit from this.

But there has been a price to pay. Around the time of Jon's death, I read about the notion of the Atlas Syndrome, identified by the psychiatrist Tim Cantopher. Named after Atlas in Greek mythology who carried the world on his shoulders, it recognised that men who were trying to hold down highly responsible jobs while simultaneously building meaningful relationships with their children were suffering seriously from stress and depression. In the 1970s the average father with children younger than five spent an estimated 15 minutes per day with them.[3] The personal and societal expectations on men in the early 2000s were very different, especially if their partner was also working part or full time – active involvement in tea, bath and bedtime routines during the week, and hours of family time at the weekend, were all part of the fathering deal.[4]

Dr Cantopher noted that the men who struggled most with juggling all of these balls were the high-achieving ones who in their usual working lives could resolve issues and troubleshoot with ease, who by their nature saw things through to the end. The less resilient, less emotionally 'strong' men who got fed up with their work/baby balance either complained about it, or delegated the baby bits to someone else. So the men who were being seen by GPs with symptoms of stress or depression tended to be the most conscientious workers or professionals who were also trying to be the best possible fathers.

RITES OF PASSAGE

Why do some men struggle to find a comfortable place in the adult world? Beyond the cultural and social transformations mentioned so far, one thing lacking in many Western cultures today is some form of rite of passage (arguably as relevant for girls as for boys). Childhood drifts into teenagerhood, which drifts into adulthood. This is not necessarily a bad thing, unless a young person finds themselves suddenly in the adult world without a real sense of how to handle themselves or behave in it. With supportive and encouraging parents, who allow increasing and age-appropriate amounts of responsibility, young men or women stand a good

---

3 See *The Scotsman*, 25 August 2003. www.scotsman.com/news/uk/burden-of-new-manhood-leads-to-depressing-rise-of-atlas-syndrome-1-661800.

4 See *The Independent*, 24 August 2003. www.independent.co.uk/life-style/health-and-families/health-news/when-being-perfect-is-just-too-much-britains-superdads-start-to-blow-a-fuse-101640.html.

chance of managing this transition. But there are many who 'get lost', or don't manage the journey between the two so well. In many cultures, rites of passage still exist, for girls as well as boys, and it is the transition into manhood from boyhood which seems to be crucial to men's sense of self in those cultures.

Most of the rites I've ever read about involve tolerating significant pain, extreme hallucinogenic drugs, or risking potentially serious injury or death. Some are genuinely too stomach-churning to include here. Hallucinogens are used by numerous tribes to various purposes – to force out memories of childhood in order to move forward into manhood, to expel evil spirits or to put the man in touch with his inner self or connect with the rest of his tribe. Much vomiting and other bodily expulsions necessarily go along with these.[5]

In Vanuatu in the South Pacific, Land Jumping is in fact not much to do with the land, but instead involves jumping from a 100-foot wooden tower suspended by a vine, which may or may not be longer than the 100 foot tower – like bungee jumping but without any health and safety regulations, and no bounce. It's a test of courage. Or insanity. Boys begin practising at the age of seven or eight from shorter towers. Their mothers hold toys or other items to represent childhood, and once the boy completes the jump, they throw the toy away to indicate the transition into the next phase of life.

The boys of the Satere-Mawe tribe in the Brazilian Amazon begin their initiation into manhood at 13. Poisonous bullet ants are sedated by the men of the tribe and sewn into large gloves. When the ants start to awaken, the boys have to wear the gloves for ten minutes – being bitten by the naturally ferocious, and by now seriously cross, ants without making a sound or showing any pain. This is repeated numerous times over the next few months. Stoicism is valued in the adult male tribe.

5　See www.artofmanliness.com or https://goodmenproject.com.

The Masai of Eastern Africa plan for the transition into manhood over many years. Sometime between the ages of 10 and 20, boys will move to live in a warrior camp, built specially for the purpose. The night before the initiation ceremony, the boys spend the night sleeping out in the forest. On the morning of the ceremony they drink a mixture of alcohol, cow's blood and milk, and eat vast quantities of meat. They are then circumcised in front of the whole tribe, when they must not flinch in pain. For up to ten years following this, the boys stay in the warrior camp, learning the skills of the hunters and warriors from the adult men, and are prepared practically for all aspects of adult life.

The Aboriginal walkabout in Australia mixes learning practical skills with making connections with spirit ancestors. The Jewish Bar Mitzvah ceremony recognises that at the age of 13 boys are old enough to take moral responsibility for themselves, although they are only adults in terms of being able to marry or get a job at the age of 18 or 20.

Even the long defunct British National Service could be seen as a rite of passage in some ways: taking a recognised path in life, male bonding, learning skills and discipline. Granted, there remain many arguments against it, not least its compulsory nature. And the imposition of raging mad poisonous ants on young boy's hands, or of public circumcisions, are also unpalatable to my delicate Western sensibilities. But I can't help but admire the value of these rites in that they mark a change from a boy's early years to the start of his adult life, with the support and oversight of older men who care about him. A little boy, maybe until the age of six or seven, needs unconditional care and love, but the gender of the primary care-giver is unimportant.[6] After that the input from his father or other close male mentors becomes an increasingly important factor in his upbringing, to ensure he reaches his potential – emotionally, socially and academically. Sadly, in British culture, this was traditionally the time when a lot of fathers started to distance themselves from

---

6   Biddulph, S. (2008) *Raising Boys*. New York: Harper Thorsons.

their sons. They would maybe go and stand on the touchline at weekends to watch them play football or rugby as they got older, but pulled back from any meaningful, emotional connection.

According to Jon this is what happened between him and his father. I don't know precisely what passed between them, but the message Jon was left with was that fathers and sons shouldn't have a close emotional relationship, and can't talk about emotional issues. And he was very clear that this happened between boys and their dads at around the age of eight. He learnt from me over years of us talking about it that this was not inevitable, and I know that one of the only good bits of his life, latterly, was thinking about all the things he could do with the children as they got older. But it was such an internalised belief in his own life, that it had coloured his whole emotional experience and his understanding of how men should communicate. How different things might have been for him if – as he'd got older – he'd been raised to understand that it was OK to express emotional stuff with your dad. That no matter how bad he felt, his dad would listen, and soak it up and make it better if he could. Or that he could find a shared passion with him, or at least something he wouldn't mind doing together occasionally – and this would be another part of the glue holding the relationship together. Having seen his dad and him together over the years, I have no doubt his dad wished they had had the emotional mechanism to do this too.

WHY JON?

Jon didn't leave a note the day he died, so we never had a definitive reason for his final action. I do have a letter he wrote to me for my birthday, five days earlier. He gave me a beautiful Victorian writing-slope box, and – as was apparently traditional – left a letter in it. On that day, it seemed like a heartfelt love letter. He told me how much, despite his 'moods and ill-thought out actions' he loved me and felt blessed by the arrival of our 'two wonderful children'.

Since he died, I've always felt that that was his 'note'. Jon's was not a spontaneous, spur of the moment suicide. I believe he had thought about it for a long time. He made a previous attempt on his life, in late 1989, when we were friends but not a couple and had he not been found by his flatmate, would have died. He always said that attempt was in response to experiences he had when travelling in Cambodia earlier in 1989. The country was still reeling from the chaos of the years of Khmer Rouge control, and intrusion by foreign powers with vested interests. As with other aspects of Jon's life, I'm not clear about exactly what he experienced when he was there, but it seems that he undertook work with charities to support local communities in their practical and emotional rebuilding. There was still in-fighting between various factions, and he seemed to have been witness to or directly involved in some of this.

On his return home, after more travels in Thailand and Australia, he apparently wrote some articles about his experiences in Cambodia. It was the repercussions of doing so which he said led him to make the first attempt on his life. When we got together in early 1992, the experience of this was still raw. He talked about it often, albeit in shorthand – I know he always sought to keep the worst details from me, but there were a select few friends with whom he chose to share more. He had been diagnosed with post-traumatic stress disorder (PTSD), and the closeness to the surface of all he had been through was tangible in those early years of our relationship. I remember one conversation, driving home from a weekend with friends in England, when it was clear things might be getting serious between us. He warned me that 'this will all come out again sometime in the future'. I took this to mean that he might need to get professional help at some point, and I reassured him that I'd try to support him however I could with whatever he might go through. With the wisdom of hindsight I think he was telling me he might sometime make another attempt on his life.

He never said so explicitly though. In the last two years of his life when he was quite often low and contemplative, he would say, 'Don't worry, I'm not going to do anything stupid.' On reflection, I suspect this meant he didn't see suicide as a stupid option: as a high achieving, problem-solving, strong-willed man, I believe he viewed it as the most logical solution to a situation which he found intolerable.

But what was so intolerable? Unlike for those of us looking in and trying to make sense of why someone would take their own life, for the suffering person there is no balance sheet of good versus bad bits of life – and if the good bits outweigh the bad, surely the only option is life? Although the person involved may think it is a clear decision, it is not the decision of a rational or well person.

One thing not right for Jon was his work. He had gone into the Bank on a graduate training programme and worked up to being on the management programme in their 'Risk and Compliance' section. For all his spirit of adventure, he was also innately conservative and conformist, and being in the Bank fitted with the latter. He was good at it. He was conscientious and competent. He got on with his colleagues and was, I think, earmarked as 'one to watch'. But he hated it in many ways. He didn't like the politics of the business world, and felt increasingly and unwillingly drawn into it. He felt that every step up the ladder tightened the 'golden handcuffs' – the company car, the other perks. He wanted to be the strong breadwinner for his family, and to create financial security, but felt trapped by his life in a career in which he felt he couldn't be true to himself.

He often talked about the possibility of moving up north and doing something more 'honest' or authentic: outdoor education, or building wooden boats. He'd have loved both. And he would have been good at both – jobs where he could have used his physicality and embraced his love of the hills or the water. And I often told him that we should do it, that nothing was more important than him finding the right path for himself. But he couldn't see beyond the need to maintain a secure financial foundation for the children, and wasn't prepared to risk it on an unconventional job.

The idea of the Atlas Syndrome rang bells with me. Jon loved being Eilidh's dad, and was desperate to be a good father to her and Cameron, but felt so constrained by the conventionality of his job that he couldn't see a way to balance these two areas of his life.

And for all Jon's bluff, macho, bravado stances, he was sensitive and emotionally astute. He often allied himself with people who were vulnerable in different ways, and could be compassionate and loyal to the most unexpected people. He also felt injustices – poverty, disability, prejudice, the state of the world – very strongly.

I think his choice to end his life was an accumulation of many issues beyond these two: his frustration over feeling he couldn't express or resolve his emotional experiences, stemming from his childhood; the stress of flashbacks and panic attacks he'd been having about Cambodia; constant pain from an ear infection which stemmed from his scuba-diving days, and which was causing him sleepless nights, worsened by what I now believe was a deep-seated depression. I think this all added to an inexorable sense of his control of life collapsing.

There were so many contradictions in Jon – his wide and varied interests, and his sometimes apparently opposing values and priorities. Throughout our relationship these mostly just added to the rich tapestry of the life we shared. But more confounding were the swings from one extreme to another in his perception of what was going on in our relationship. At times he was so cold and distant I felt overwhelmed by loneliness. At others, his insight into his behaviour was remarkable. I remember watching the 1940s Gothic thriller *Gaslight*, about a man who manipulates his wife into believing she is going mad. Jon clearly felt uncomfortable during the film and afterwards said, 'I've played those kinds of mind games with you, haven't I?' I don't believe he was trying to induce madness in me, but I do now think his own troubled state of mind led him to take some of his frustration (or whatever it was) out on me because I was closest to him. Or maybe he was trying to test me to see how strong I was. I don't think he could have explained it anyway. But it served to emphasise the constant struggle that was clearly going on inside him, revealed through his constantly changing behaviour towards me.

In the last months of his life, when I was pregnant with Cameron, our relationship increasingly swung between extremes dictated by his moods. He was sometimes cold and rejecting, and when I suggested we talk about things, he said there was nothing to talk about and maybe we should get divorced if I was so unhappy. At other times, he was overtly low and worried, desperately trying to find a way through the stress he was feeling – and at those times he was open and communicative. I felt a sense of hope that because we were talking openly and honestly, we might be able to find a solution. After years of often being emotionally shut out, I felt grateful for this apparent way in to help him, to be able to show how much I loved him, and for this to apparently be reciprocated. Stupid, really. In retrospect, those must have been the worst of times for him, when none of my reassurances or support for his plans to change direction in his life would have made any difference. I think he was desperate to hear me say them, but was actually so vulnerable and too far down the road of 'there's no way out of this' for my words to have any impact. He refused to see the doctor or anyone else to discuss any of it. His experience in the psychiatric hospital in 1989 had convinced him never to go anywhere near professional help again – not an indictment of psychiatrists, but an indication that he was unprepared and unable to lay himself open and exposed to anyone else. As I've said, the message that 'boys don't cry' or discuss their feelings had been hard-wired in him.

A few months after Jon died I met with Louis Appleby, a medical colleague of my dad's. In recent years he has been the head of the National Suicide Prevention Strategy for England, and at that time was involved in advising Tony Blair's Government about the issues involved in male suicide. I was trying to make sense of what had happened, and what in Jon's background and life might have led to his suicide, and am eternally grateful to Professor Appleby for his clarity and ability to assimilate all the information I verbally threw at him that day. As well as the events leading up to Jon's death I told him about the history of alcoholism and mental health issues in various members of his paternal family. I also mentioned his tendency throughout his life to live on the edge, doing risky sports, striving for excellence and having very high expectations of himself and those around him, and also his refusal to suffer fools gladly. I told him about Cambodia and the first attempt Jon made on his life. And I explained the mix in him of emotionally pragmatic coldness balanced at times by huge sensitivity, compassion and emotional insight.

Professor Appleby said that, based on this admittedly brief history, he suspected that Jon might have had an underlying genetic predisposition to depression, which might have been bubbling at a low level throughout his life. He said that although Jon's experiences in Cambodia were challenging and his reaction authentic, this seemed to be a red herring insofar as he did not believe it was the cause of his mental health issues, although it was certainly a trigger for them to come to the surface.

He said he felt that the type of underlying depression Jon had may have led him to take his own life at some point, if not when he did, then later. He emphasised the issue for some high-achieving men – who are used to being able to solve problems in professional or other aspects of their lives – is that when they face a situation, often emotional or personal, for which they can find no solution, they can become overwhelmed by this. Professor Appleby suggested that Jon might have been planning his suicide for some time, and agreed that perhaps an accumulation of circumstances had finally led him to kill himself. He said the loss of hope (or any glimmer of optimism, as I see it) is the determining factor for most people who take their own lives. And he said there is often a final straw – even the speeding ticket Jon got three days before he died might have been sufficient to break the camel's back. In itself it was trivial, but in Jon's eyes it was the last intolerable burden added to the already insurmountable pile.

MIND-KNOTS AND MAKING SENSE
In the weeks after Jon died, and even more so after my meeting with Louis Appleby, I came to think of Jon as a ticking time bomb that would have exploded at some point, regardless of what anybody tried to do to help him. It felt as if he had been on a trajectory

which could not be altered – and in some ways, this made it easier for me to start trying to make some sense of what had happened, and to believe that I could have done nothing more to prevent his final action. I have never felt angry with him, although I know many friends did, for 'leaving us' like he did. I only ever felt love and compassion for him, because his pain must have been so unutterably awful.

Over the years, I have also made sense of the aspects of our relationship which often undermined me at the time – the mind games, the temper, the untruths. They weren't constant, but worrying about his reactions all the time made me feel as if I was walking on eggshells. Now I believe these behaviours were all symptoms of his illness, and that the dis-ease that is depression, which made Jon feel such deep dissatisfaction with himself, led him to take it out on me, who was closest to him.

I wonder whether if Jon had known what his family's lives would end up being, he'd have made a different decision. If he could have seen what it's been like for the children without their dad, if he had known I hadn't ended up meeting someone else to share my life with, if he could have seen his parents' and brother's pain. Most of the time, though, I don't really think he would have done anything differently, because what I understand about suicide is that there's little rational thought involved. For the person, at the time, it seems like the clearest decision, and for Jon, I absolutely believe he thought it was the right decision and the best one for us. I know it wasn't – but for him, who couldn't see a solution to whatever intractable problems he felt he was facing, it was the only way to resolve them. As I've said, there isn't a balance sheet – 'there are more good things than bad, so I won't kill myself' – and there isn't an ability to say, 'things feel bad today, but look at all the good things that are around me, and when I feel better, they're there for the taking'. The thing about suicide is that there is no hope. There is no belief in better things to come. That's why it seems like the most sensible thing to do.

Eilidh often asks what it would have been like if Jon were still here, what kind of dad he'd have been. This is impossible to answer, because if he were still here, he'd still be unwell, still have mental health issues. And so although I feel sad to think about all the brilliant things he could have done with our children, there would also have been times of stress and dispute and tension, and they would likely have lived with the same uncertainty about his moods and learned to tread carefully and walk on eggshells as I did.

But of course, the truth is actually much clearer than any of this: He died because he made that choice. To him it was the rational solution to a problem he found intolerable. Any thoughts of 'what if he'd survived' are purely hypothetical...it's like a mind game that wraps your brain in knots, because it's simply not plausible or possible. I think he didn't leave a note because no explanation or justification would actually have helped, or made a difference. Or mitigate the fact that he took his own life. And I respect the clarity of that decision.

But every day – despite the mind-knots involved, less so now for my sake, but always for the children's sake – I wish it had been different.

CHAPTER 7

TALKING TO THE CHILDREN

Louis Appleby advised me to tell the children how Jon died as soon as possible. He said children can cope with any information so long as it is given in language they understand, and in as safe and reassuring a way as possible. In my rational head, my social-work head, I understood and firmly believed this. I have worked with adoptive, kinship and foster carers for many years, and absolutely believe in children knowing and understanding the details of their stories from as early an age as possible. The notion of, as in years gone by, an 18-year-old discovering for the first time by accident that the people they regarded as their parents were in fact their adoptive parents, has thankfully not been part of social work practice (or good sense) for a long time. Letting children grow up with their life story – given to them in safe, small steps, in words and pictures that are reassuring and age-appropriate – is best practice, and I believe has the child's best interests at heart.

Similarly, I have seen friends whose child was diagnosed with Asperger's Syndrome, who have shared the meaning of this with him, and the implications of it for him, from the earliest age. Their other children knew and understood about it, and so from the youngest ages, could make sense of their brother's behaviour, and have some understanding of why he was sometimes treated differently from them. All of this meant that as individuals and as a family they could access the best possible support and advice, and crucially there were never any secrets about his condition. Perhaps most importantly, he has grown up knowing that the Asperger's is a valuable part of who he is…it doesn't define him, but it is part of him, and acknowledging its existence makes him his true self.

In any of these situations, or in the case of bereavement, I have always believed that honesty and not hiding from the truth, is the healthiest and most positive approach. It means that the children's stories or situations are hopefully not scary or traumatic, but become over the years a diminishing mystery (and to be honest, this applies to adults too). If they know the truth from the earliest possible stage, all that can then happen is that they build a better and fuller understanding at each developmental stage. This isn't to say that this is easy, and I know people who have chosen not to share vital parts of a child's story with them, whether this is about a loss, or a diagnosis, or their pre-care history. For many people a very real fear of 'not wanting to upset' the child, or another family member, can be a huge obstacle to being honest, and is understandable. But these *are* upsetting issues, and to keep them or our feelings about them hidden away beneath a hard and defended outer shell is not self-protective; it is ultimately self-destructive. What can a child learn about living an emotionally fulfilled life from being shown that they should never get upset, or learn how to resolve that upset?

I know some people feel that once the information or the story is out in the child's world, the genie is out of the lamp, and that it is better to keep it in there. My parents-in-law were firmly of that belief, and couldn't understand why I thought it was necessary to share the nature of Jon's death with Cameron and Eilidh. Part of me understood this. I would much rather I'd never had to be faced with the dilemma of when to tell my young children their father had chosen to kill himself. The thought of doing it made me feel sick. Until I told them, it felt as if they still had the innocence that comes with not knowing that people can make such a choice. But once that knowledge was in their heads, I felt – rightly – that their lives and understanding of the world would be changed forever.

But that was no reason not to tell them. It was their information to own and know – the longer I didn't tell them was more time that they had to construct a false version of events, and longer, eventually, that we would have to unpick that falsehood when they did finally hear the truth.

Eilidh was always a child who asked questions. One of the best was when she was four and asked me where the first ever baby came from. Talk about throwing me back on my understanding of Darwinism and evolution – and trying to pull together an answer in language for a pre-schooler!

As she got older, she talked and asked a lot about Jon. As I said earlier, she always had her own memories of him – not just the stories that friends and family and I told about him. And she struggled with doing things at weekends or on holiday when there were always lots of dads around with their own families.

Cameron had no memories of Jon, but as a little boy – vying as siblings do for whose experience was the biggest/worst/best – he used to say it was worse for him because at least Eilidh did remember their dad. Personally, I think it was just horrible for both of them. Cameron didn't really ask much about Jon, but Eilidh always did. And as time went by, her questions became more searching. The story I had always told was as close to the truth as I could get. I said that their dad had been walking on Arthur's Seat, and slipped when he got too close to the edge. By the time she was six, Eilidh had started asking me why that had happened, because 'Daddy was a really good hillwalker'.

I knew I had to tell them the truth soon, because I didn't want to get into a knot of half-truths. The longer time went by, I was also concerned that some information might somehow come out at school, or in our circle of friends. I carefully thought out my plan – the Easter break was approaching and I felt it would be best to tell the children at the start of the holiday so we would have a couple of weeks together when they didn't need to be at school, so they could process the story and ask me anything they needed to after breaking the news. I wanted to tell them on a sunny day, and in the open air, so I waited for the first good day, and decided to go to one of the old castles near us in East Lothian. The best laid plans, etc. etc.

Even though she was only seven, Eilidh was beside herself that I'd 'lied' to her until then. She cried, and calmed down, and cried again. She was confused about why Jon could have done such a thing 'because he always seemed so happy'. I told her that he often *was* happy, that he loved being her daddy, and having a baby boy, but that the illness he had meant there were times when he felt very sad as well, but that he was brave, and managed to hide this from her. It was the first of many, many conversations over the years when I realised I would have to try and make sense of the unimaginable and inexplicable for my children, and I felt the weight of having to get it as right as possible for them. Eilidh has refused to ever go back to the castle where I shared Jon's story with them.

The only light relief that day came when Cameron, aged five, said of his dad's suicide, 'Well that was a silly thing to do'. Out of the mouths of babes...

HELPING THE CHILDREN TO BUILD RESILIENCE

My planning, to have the whole Easter holiday to mop up any emotional backlash, didn't seem to be necessary. Once the facts were out in their world, the children appeared to carry on as usual. But of course, they were processing the story in their own ways, and the questions and demands for more information came out at unexpected and unpredictable times over the weeks and months and years to follow. That's life. We can't plan for emotional events, or how we will deal with them. Managing my children's grief and loss in the past 15 years has made me draw on the deepest reserves of good sense and wisdom and careful language – and I'm not really a consistently sensible, wise or carefully-spoken person. But I have always known that anything to do with stories of their dad has to be handled incredibly sensitively, and honestly.

My priority, the constant subtext to our lives since Jon died, has been for me to protect the children from the legacy of his mental health problems. By which I mean not just the tragedy of the choice he made and the loss of their dad, but the importance for them of knowing how to face the emotional challenges of life in a confident way. It is not unusual for children who have a parent who has taken their own life to worry that they might do the same thing, or to struggle with mental health issues. It is a horrible fear to live with, and almost from the day Jon died, I knew that I would do anything to try and reassure them that they can live their lives differently to their dad.

They already had a greater understanding of death and loss than many people significantly older than they had. I had never worried about talking about their dad, sharing stories about him, or talking about what happens when someone dies in a way that hopefully made sense to them. I found some great children's books to read with them which told stories about family, friends or pets who died, using wonderful child-centred language. This all meant that from their earliest years, Eilidh and Cameron didn't find the subject of death taboo. It wasn't that it was a good thing, or something they relished talking about, but they were growing up with an honest understanding of the idea that people can stop being here with us, and with their children's comprehension, they accepted this.

Eilidh's nursery teacher (who was aware that Jon had died) called me aside one day when I went to collect her. She explained that they had been talking about daddies that morning in anticipation of Father's Day, and Eilidh had told the other children that her daddy was dead. One little boy had apparently looked confused and asked, 'Is your daddy a sausage?' Eilidh had looked incredulous and said, 'No, he's in Heaven' (the explanation we used at that time), as if, surely everyone knew that. The nursery teacher had wanted to tell me in case Eilidh came out with a seemingly random story about sausages.

The only sense I could make of the sausage incident was that the little boy's only knowledge of death was maybe from a dinner-time conversation, having asked his parents where a sausage came from, and they told him that when a pig dies it is made into sausages. Any other explanation, really, is beyond my imagination!

WINSTON'S WISH

What the incident with the sausage made very clear to me was that my own children's understanding of death and loss was well in advance of their years. However, the issues involved in death by suicide were much more complex, and once I had shared the details of Jon's death with them, I was aware that I needed some external support to help them start to make better sense of it. An early part of this process was for us to make contact with Winston's Wish. They are a UK national bereavement charity, and work with children and their families to support them through their loss of a loved one.

I had read quite a bit about the organisation before first making contact, and was aware that they have particular experience in working with the families of people who have died by suicide. I wasn't really sure what I was looking for in terms of support, but I hoped that connecting with other children who had been through similar experiences would be helpful for Eilidh and Cameron. Over the years since Jon died I had read about various support organisations, wondering if I should get involved with them, but I'd never actually done it. Partly that was because I had lots of friends and family and we had a busy social life, so how was I going to fit in meeting more people? But probably, more honestly, I was unsure about joining a group who were all defined by their bereavement, or their single parenthood. Because Jon had died, I was eligible to be part of both groups, but I hadn't been ready to make that a public statement, and I suppose I wanted to hold on to the fact that I was also still just me. But now, for the children's sakes, it seemed that allying ourselves with other families in a similar situation was the right thing to do.

Our experience of Winston's Wish, and all the people who work there, was unfailingly positive. From the outset, I was struck by the kindness, sensitivity and concern shown to us by everyone we met, without being sugary or smothering. They were experts in dealing with families' loss and pain, and they conveyed that expertise in their open and generous support and care for us. We met first at their offices in Cheltenham, for an intense day of getting to know each other and sharing the story of Jon's death. Their theory, tested through years of experience, is that children can best make sense of their loss if they understand all the details of what happened, including the circumstances leading up to the death. This also ensured that everyone in the family had exactly the same knowledge and understanding of what happened, and that there were no secrets.

I thought I'd done a fairly good job of telling Jon's story, and handling this as carefully as possible. But on the day, I realised that I had never mentioned his first suicide attempt after his experiences in Cambodia. This wasn't a deliberate omission – it had just never seemed relevant when, to me, his death had been the most important part of the story. In fact, I hadn't thought about how to tell the children since before he died. After his first suicide attempt he was left with visible scars. Before Jon died I used to wonder how and when we would have to explain the scars to Eilidh and Cameron. Afterwards, there was never going to be a time when they'd ask those questions, because they would never see them.

However, now I had to tell them for the first time, and although the Winston's staff were completely supportive, I felt as if I had made a terrible mistake by not letting them know earlier. Actually, from where I stand now, I don't think this was too unforgivable – as part of Jon's longer story, it was important for the children to know, and on the day, Eilidh was shocked, and upset that she hadn't known before. But I haven't beaten myself up about it too much. It simply served to emphasise that any 'secrets', even unintentional ones, have no place in completely honest and open relationships, and that they will usually, if not inevitably, come out at some later point.

Following that day we had a couple of months to wait before being allocated places on one of the Winston's Wish weekend camps. The children spent the two days with other children who had been bereaved by suicide. I spent them with the other parents (as mentioned in Chapter 5, all women). I had been so focused on finding the right kind of support for the children it had never occurred to me that spending time with other parents would be supportive or beneficial for me. As it turned out, it was an unexpectedly life-affirming experience for me. Being with people who absolutely knew exactly what we had been through, because they had been through it, too, was a revelation. I felt like I did when Eilidh was first born – that I'd chanced upon a club (parenthood with Eilidh; bereaved by suicide at Winston's) in which I felt utterly comfortable, but about whose existence I'd been totally ignorant until that point. In our group we did a lot of the activities that the children were doing in their groups – helpful for us, but also in order to understand what they had been going through.

The staff who facilitated our group were protective, caring and broad-shouldered in sharing the pain that was raw and anguished at times during the weekend. I know that the children's helpers were equally skilled. Having had no expectations about our own camp, we were all overwhelmed by the kindness of our group workers – the constant provision of lovely food, an overnight stay in a beautiful Georgian country house, and an evening of complementary therapies. To have a night away from the children, knowing they were being well cared for, while being so nurtured ourselves was a rare experience for most of us. Amidst the grief and sadness, we made connections, and at the start of what became friendships between a few of us which have lasted, we all realised, for the first time, the benefit of being with people who implicitly understood our backstories. These are the friends with whom I was able to share the most painful aspects of Jon's death, because they knew exactly what that was like, and we didn't need to protect each other as I think we all felt the need with other people in our lives. But we could also be together and not always refer to the children's fathers, because the understanding of our situations was implicit.

At the end of the weekend there was a ceremony at the children's camp, when they performed songs they had practised and shared some of the work they had done, and we released balloons over the Gloucestershire countryside for all the people who had died. Seeing Cameron and Eilidh with that group of children who had all lost a parent or other relative to suicide was oddly overwhelming and wonderful at the same time. For years since Jon died I had felt that they were living in a world which had no idea about what they had been through, but now they had found a club (like I had) which understood completely.

Afterwards, it was apparent that the experience had meant different things to Eilidh and Cameron. He was only seven at the time, and, as I've said before, has expressed his feelings about Jon's death differently, less explicitly, than Eilidh over the years. Even now, as a teenager, his chosen approach to emotional expression is 'as and when needed', and I think, in retrospect, the Winston's Wish camp came at a time when Eilidh needed it, but he didn't. I think it helped him to see that other children were in a similar situation, but his need for emotional solace or supportive structures at that exact time was less than hers. She, on the other hand, aged nine, seemed to have gained strength and confidence from meeting children in the same situation.

The weekend was the start of a new phase of the children's path through their grief. It will, being realistic, take them throughout their lives – their dad's suicide will be part of them forever. But what they learned in that safe setting – that they could talk about it, and share their feelings about it with people other than me – set them off on that path in as positive a way as possible.

HOW TO TALK ABOUT DEATH AND DYING WITH CHILDREN

It feels like the hardest thing in the world. And it is one of the hardest. There has never been a time when I haven't wished I didn't need to do it. Because every conversation, every question the children have asked, have reminded me that they are living their life without their dad. It stinks. I would love never to have had all the conversations, beyond count, that we've had over the years.

And I do understand why some people's reaction to the death of a loved one, let alone the suicide, might be to avoid talking about it – to talk about it in platitudes or safe one-liners. Or not actually talk about it at all. It is really painful: it's painful for the children, it's painful for the parent or other care-givers – and as a parent, isn't what we do to try and protect our children from pain? And how do we actually answer the questions that the children might ask?

Because every time they do, it raises all our own memories as powerfully and starkly as if they had just happened. And the truth of what happened is probably the most painful thing that has happened to us, and self-preservation normally keeps us away from things that cause us pain.

But not talking about it doesn't make the pain any less. It doesn't make what happened not happen. And by not talking honestly with children, the most likely thing to happen is that they will imagine things which are possibly even worse than the truth. And they will know that you haven't been honest with them, even if you believe you have been doing so to protect them. Most children are innately curious, and are astute judges of character and situations. They are especially astute when it comes to their parents, and will intuit if something doesn't feel right. How can we expect our children to be truthful if we hide the truth of the most significant part of their lives from them? The information about whoever died is as much theirs as it is ours. It may be the worst thing we ever have to tell them, but that's no reason to keep it from them. And the sooner they know about the story, the more time they have to understand it and start trying to make sense of it. Over time, as I've said, it can become a diminishing mystery, rather than the hugest elephant in the room if you don't talk openly about it. And while going through life with the knowledge of their parent's death will continue to be painful, it will be so much less if you can walk honestly along that path beside them and carry the load together.

From the outset, I wanted to be as honest with the children as possible, within the limits of their age and their ability to understand. I decided that if they asked a question about Jon I would answer as directly and honestly as I could, using words that would make sense to them. I would tell them as much as they needed to know within truthful limits, but no more. Children will always ask more questions if they're not satisfied with your first answer. They are the best guide possible as to whether or not you've said enough, or said it clearly enough. If you've ever tried to distract a curious four-year-old with the bit between her teeth from an awkward or searching conversation, you will know what I mean.

When faced with having to add a bit more to the story of Jon's death it helped me to be clear in my own head about which aspects I wanted to share with the children, and what kind of words I could use with them. I often subconsciously rehearsed things in anticipation of the next questions arising. This meant trying to make sense for myself of what had happened so that I could give Eilidh and Cameron the clearest explanation whenever they asked, which probably helped me through my own grieving process.

When the children were very young, there were some lovely books to read with them about loss and grief. Our favourites were *Badger's Parting Gifts* by Susan Varley, *The Sunshine Cat* by Miriam Moss and *Heaven* by Nicholas Allan. They all deal with animals and their losses, but they talk about many of the feelings and emotions that can result from any bereavement. Lots of other children's books deal with loving and caring, and could as easily be applied to a relationship with someone who is no longer here as they could to the surviving parent or care-giver. We were even able to read books about dads because they allowed us to remember good and funny bits about Jon. The skill of the writers and illustrators of children's books helped us to work through a lot of difficult and powerful emotions in a safe and unthreatening way, and I gratefully added their offerings to the repertoire of words I used to help the children work their way through the loss of their dad.

Sometimes words are not the most important part of remembering the person who has died. There is no right or wrong way to remember them – only the way that feels right for you all. Personally, I have never wanted to make a big deal of the day Jon died. It was the worst day of my life and the less attention we draw to it the better. I regard it as a random date when he chose to end his life, and although I am always aware of it when it comes, I refuse to dignify it with any momentousness. What we've done instead over the years is to remember Jon at lots of different times. I wanted the children to grow up with stories and memories of him which were about the brilliant life he lived, and not tied to the day he died.

So we have visited places he loved and done things he loved doing. Any hills we climb or beaches we walk on, or curries we eat,

I regard as being in honour of him. The bookcases at home still hold many of the books he read and referred to, and although they're undoubtedly outdated now (mostly bought secondhand years ago, so old even at the time!) they tell the story of him and his widely varied enthusiasms. Our friendships with the people he also loved and cared for are even more precious because he used to be part of them.

MARKING IMPORTANT DAYS

At different times in their lives, Eilidh and Cameron have wanted to do different things to remember their dad on important days – mostly his birthday and Father's Day. For a long time we remembered his birthday with a party tea and cake – I suspect as much because the children enjoyed it as needing to do it in memory of their dad. But whatever the reason, it was important for them that we did it. We sometimes lit a candle for him, and always told stories about him. On Father's Day, we often wrote messages for him (and after much trial and error discovered that airmail paper is best, because it's lightest) and tied them to balloons which we would let go and watch until they disappeared from sight.

As the children have got older, we haven't done such specific things, probably because the way we include stories or anecdotes about him has long been a natural part of everyday life. It was important to do them when the children were young, so that they had a positive activity in memory of Jon, and to remind us all that we hadn't forgotten him. With age and maturity and emotional intelligence, I think they know he is part of their lives without needing to resort to these any more. But any memory exercise that makes you or your children feel connected to your loved one has validity, no matter how long after your loss. The way we have moved through the last 15 years has been about what has felt right for us. Other people, I know, have continued to use memory boxes or candles, or other things, to provide more tangible reminders of the person they lost. There is a list of some exercises and details of the organisations that have helped us and can provide much more support with other such activities in the Appendix.

I have often thought about whether or not we should have had some kind of formal memorial for Jon. Some friends have planted trees for their loved one. Others have used traditional headstones or plaques. Whatever physical memorial exists, it can be a place where memories of the person can be focussed and uninterrupted. We took Jon's ashes to a beautiful place beside a waterfall which had great significance for us. There isn't a plaque or anything specific to alert other people to it, but I like to think, after 15 years, that the foliage and trees and everything else there is more thriving, and a brighter shade of green than the surrounding areas. We make sure we go at least once a year, and sit on the bench nearby, and nowadays just tend to have a chat while feeling close to him. One year, hopefully, we might even remember the can of beer we keep promising to bring for him...

WHAT TO SHARE AT SCHOOL

On top of being open with the children in our own relationships, I was also keen to keep their schools informed about any relevant issues regarding their dad's death, so their teachers could be appropriately supportive. I know, having talked with our friends from Winston's Wish, that people feel very differently about how to manage this. For my part, I was always guided by the children. At primary school, where they only had one class teacher per year, the information about Jon's suicide was passed from one teacher to the other at the year start, and I spoke with any who I didn't already know to explain how Eilidh and Cameron were likely to react. Without exception, they were all sensitive and supportive, especially when events such as Father's Day cropped up, and after we had our Winston's Wish weekend camp. We were lucky to have such emotionally intelligent teachers, who seemed to take their cues from Eilidh and Cameron about how much or little to discuss.

When Eilidh moved to high school, she didn't want all her subject teachers to know about her dad. She decided we should just tell her guidance teacher, and it would be up to them in discussion together to decide if she wanted to share the information more widely. For the most part this has worked out well. As she has gone through the school and developed closer relationships with some teachers, she has chosen to share the details of Jon's death with them anyway. The only exceptions to 'working out well' concerned Religious and Moral Education and Modern Studies classes dealing with euthanasia. In the first, the teacher prepared the class for the film beforehand, explaining the explicit nature of the coverage, but she didn't know Eilidh's circumstances. Eilidh found the graphic details of the film upsetting, and the teacher responded completely appropriately by talking it through with her and excusing her from all further euthanasia discussions. The second incident was really a near miss: Eilidh's Modern Studies teacher showed his other class a very graphic film dealing with euthanasia, without preparing them for it at all. Some of Eilidh's friends found it very upsetting, despite not having lost a parent to suicide. She was shocked that the teacher was likely to present the film in the same way to her class, and so we managed to have her excused from the euthanasia section of teaching again.

Even these incidents did not persuade her to change her policy of not sharing the information about Jon's death. She rationalised them as random occurrences, highly unlikely to recur. She, and Cameron after her, felt strongly that the details of Jon's suicide were theirs to guard and share very sparingly with the people they trusted most, and this seems to have stood them both in good stead. This has applied to friends as well as teachers. For years, almost none of their school friends knew how Jon died. Gradually, I think as they have found a way of telling the story which feels safe for them, they have told more of their close circles of friends, but by no means all of them. For Cameron this might partly be to do with not wanting to be defined by Jon's absence. For Eilidh, I think she has always been very private about her own emotional issues. Whatever, I completely respect their choices to share in the way they have, and I feel confident that they can protect themselves and their story as they get older.

CHAPTER 8

RISKS FOR BEREAVED CHILDREN

The old adage that you are only ever as happy as your least happy child was not, I think, written for or by a bereaved parent. I'm sure most parents know exactly what that feels like – it's not the unique domain of those who have lost a partner. But I am aware that while it is true for me, it is also always overlaid (and I mean still, and probably for the rest of my life) with the added default assumption or worry that their unhappiness may be directly related to their dad's suicide, or – for me, worse – a symptom of a mental health vulnerability.

It isn't unusual today for children to have mental health problems. There are too many articles and reports about situations where children are experiencing stresses and pressures that have made their lives intolerable. And this is not just teenagers who have always been predisposed to emotional expression in overt or covert ways. Now, primary school children are falling prey to the high expectations of social relationships and school, or the insidious pressures of social media. This always shocks me, and I read about the cases of children's and young people's experiences of depression with increasing sadness. The notion of 'copycat' mental health issues – where children see friends or peers displaying symptoms of mental health problems or self-harming, and emulate them – has been widely reported. Whatever we think about this, if those children had positive self-esteem and confidence, they would not feel the need to do as their friends do, and they add to the picture of a nation's childhoods which are increasingly blighted by poor mental health. All of us, parents or not, should be concerned about this and mindful of trying to make a difference where we can.

Children bereaved by suicide have to live in that real world with all those outside pressures, but they also have the constant subtext of their parent's death. And some fear that they may 'do the same as they did' or, at least, be vulnerable to depression or other mental ill health. Whenever Eilidh or Cameron have had an emotional 'wobble', my head has gone first to the immediate problem, and how we might be able to work through it, but it always also goes to those deeper places where the fear of something darker resides. And it's in my head because I know it might also at times be in theirs.

This has its foundation in research evidence. The most recent information suggests that around 5 per cent of under-16s were bereaved of at least one parent in 2011. If the loss of siblings, other close relatives or friends were included, the figure rose significantly. No data is collected on the number of children bereaved of a parent by suicide in the UK, but the Child Bereavement Network cautiously estimates that it could be as many as 3000 children each year. There is considerable overlap between the emotional impact of any parental bereavement, and that of parental suicide. In general, children who lose a parent in any way are at greater risk than non-bereaved children of depression, anxiety, bullying (due to lower self-esteem), angry outbursts, drug or alcohol misuse, teenage pregnancy, regression of developmental milestones, and poorer school performance. The risk of depression can be anywhere between 50 per cent and 100 per cent greater than for those children not bereaved. For those who lose a parent to suicide, the rates of depression are at the highest level, and the risk of them taking their own life can be up to three times that of non-bereaved children.

Taken together, these outcomes seem like a doom-laden litany. But – and it is a big but – not all, or even any, are inevitable. They are all highly variable, and depend on many circumstances, some of which are outwith the surviving parent's or carer's control, but many are within our grasp. It is possible to construct a strong and resilient life for your children – easier, admittedly if they are already tough little people with good self-esteem, but not impossible. Helping to build resilience – or 'doing well in the face of adversity' – is about 'normalising grief and strengthening coping strategies'.[7] Things which can help are your own positive attitude and strong, loving attachments with your children, to give them a sense of emotional safety; strong support from your family and friends, and being able to ask for help when you need it; and having an ongoing relationship with the person who died, in the sense of keeping them alive through talking and sharing positive memories, and having photos or videos of them as part of daily life. All of these have been proven to help children make the best sense of their loss, and to develop strong coping strategies as they get older.

And while the risks for bereaved children are real, and need to be addressed throughout their lives, the positive outcomes after a bereavement should also be celebrated. These might come about partly as 'tributes' to the person who died – for instance, children taking up one of their favourite sports or focusing on their school studies to make them proud. In the way they decide to live their lives more generally, their resolve to do things differently to their parent may also be seen – a wish to live life to the full and seize every opportunity, gratitude for the lives they have, developing new interests, being ready to accept help from or offer help to others, or an ability to acknowledge their own strengths or abilities.

GIVING THEM SPACE, LISTENING CAREFULLY

The reality is that many children bereaved by suicide are a blend of these brilliant and inspired bits, plus the more vulnerable bits. These are all parts of their lost parent's legacy. The trick for them, and us as their surviving parent, is to find a way to allow them to live comfortably and healthily with the two aspects alongside each other. Over the years, Cameron and Eilidh have had emotional 'wobbles' for different reasons. My natural instinct has always been

---

7   From Robbie Gilligan, Head of the School of Social work and Social policy at Trinity College, Dublin, who has researched and written on issues of resilience for thirty years.

to try and find a reason, then try and sort it out. 'Reasons' were and are not always clear. Or simple. Or obviously connected to their dad's suicide. I soon learned that there was a big-picture version of their lives, as there is of all our lives, and over-analysing wasn't necessarily helpful. There was a problem, but the detailed causes of it were not actually the important part. Getting it sorted was. Jon's death may have been a factor in whatever problem they were having – and sometimes more so than others – but so were their own personalities and vulnerabilities, and the pressures from their everyday lives.

Some of these wobbles were bigger, more upsetting and longer-lived than others. Some had relatively simple solutions. They are, however, the children's personal emotional property, and I don't plan to discuss them here. What I will say is that each time they had a crisis, I tried to really listen to them and understand what they needed. Listening is very different to hearing, because it should lead us to an honest connection with a person's own experience, not just our idea of what their experience might be. Sometimes we could work out a plan together of what they and I thought might help. Sometimes I needed to be a bit more directive, when things for them felt particularly bleak. Eilidh and I did a lot of long beach walks during one phase – she needed to be outside and surrounded by space where we could talk without feeling constrained by four walls. We also made lots of lists to check if the 'good bits' outweighed the 'bad bits'. They usually did. And seeing things written down on paper seemed to help get them out of her head, and to resume a more balanced perspective.

Talking to Cameron in the middle of the night about anything and everything seemed to help to take his mind off the anxieties which kept him awake. And for both of them at different times, I have asked for help from wise and expert people who know more about young people's emotional lives than I do. Not only did this give Eilidh and Cameron the chance to talk about things with someone other than me, but they also learned that with other people's help they could find strategies which made things feel better, and which they will be able to use throughout their lives. For Eilidh, especially, normalising her grief has been really important. She has been involved with Richmond's Hope, a local children's bereavement organisation, for a number of years. They offer individual support and also have a teenager's group – and both of those supports, plus helping to run support groups for younger children there, have been a significant and positive part of her life. Cameron, on the other hand, hasn't wanted to become involved with them, but knows that they are there if he ever changes his mind. Another thing I have learned: you can't assume that both (or all) of your children will respond to their parent's death (or life, or anything) in the same way. As I said earlier, you need to really listen to each child, and do what they need.

GROWING UP QUICKLY

The other thing which might be glaringly obvious about children who lose a parent is that it tends to make then grow up very fast. From their earliest ages, my two have lived with the knowledge that somebody very close to them can die, and never come back. And they have lived their lives understanding, internalising and feeling what that is like, every day. I think only two other children in their circles here at home have lost a parent (plus, of course our friends from Winston's Wish). Most, thank goodness, have not. Statistically, as has been said, it is quite rare. But many children will have experienced a loss of some kind, whether it be a wider family member, a friend or a pet; some have experienced the separation of their parents, or maybe a parent's loss of a job or serious illness. All of these are life-changing events for children in different ways, as are being bullied, having a serious illness or injury themselves, or experiencing mental health difficulties. There isn't a scale of most terrible life events, or – by inference – their effect on how quickly they make a child grow up. All of these experiences will most likely lead to a way of viewing the world with more mature, or jaded, or just more realistic eyes.

I would dearly love Cameron and Eilidh never to have known that their best loved people could die, and especially not, like their dad, by his own choice. It would have been brilliant for them to have got to this stage in their teens without knowing the pain, or experiencing the related anxieties that come from such a loss.

This has practical as well as emotional implications. I have always been aware of this, but it was brought home to me when I had a minor operation in the past year. Two different friends offered to take me and bring me home from hospital, and another – because I couldn't be discharged without an adult being present overnight – had a sleepover with us. Not really as fun as it sounds, given my drugged-to-the-eyeballs state! However, after that first 24 hours, it was just me and the children, as Mum and Dad – who had planned to come and help out – were laid up with the flu. And Eilidh and Cameron managed brilliantly. I'd sorted meals beforehand, and they knew how to deal with all the practicalities in the house. But I felt guilty that they had to do all of that, while I was really no use whatsoever for three days. And worse than that, I couldn't do anything about looking a bit vulnerable and being in a fair bit of pain, which I knew concerned them.

In the end, though, any situation which they have to deal with as a result of Jon's absence can have one of two outcomes. They can either learn from it that life's curveballs are scary and unsettling, and their armour can be dented by one more degree every time they face a challenge, or – and I hope this is where they are heading – those curveballs can be well caught, and they can grow in confidence and wisdom every time they deal with them.

And I have realised that as mature and perceptive teenagers, it is OK for them to discover that I'm not infallible, and I don't always get things right, or know the answer to every problem. We got stranded one night in the middle of Berlin at 10.30pm during our summer holiday this year. The trains stopped running for some reason not mentioned in our guidebook. The solution, to get back to our apartment out of town, wasn't immediately obvious and I knew Eilidh and Cameron were aware of my cogs whirring, trying to find an alternative way back, with no staff or public messages to point the way, and an almost complete lack of German language between us. But I rationalised that they were as well equipped as me to work it out, and although I still felt the need to be calm and apparently unworried, it wasn't the same as when they were younger and the pressure to appear omnipotent and competent in every situation was much greater.

It was another life lesson for them – that there are some unpredictable situations which you just have to muddle through, even if you're a supposedly omnipotent single parent. (The solution to the lack of trains was the replacement bus service which we finally stumbled across…all fine in the end.)

And whenever Eilidh and Cameron behave like giddy, giggling, irresponsible teenagers, I feel grateful that they can do that, too. They can let go, and be joyful and irreverent and pleasure-seeking like the best of their peers. And if that goes hand in hand with their more serious cores, developed through the loss of their dad, then I think that balance will stand them in good stead for whatever comes next in their lives.

THINGS EILIDH LOVES

Surfing

Country music, especially Blake Shelton

Travelling

Curry

Camping

Geography and English

Photography

Reading

Buffy the Vampire Slayer

Hillwalking

Chocolate

Poldark

Scotland

Heat and sunshine

Making her own photoshopped cards for friend's birthdays (like Moonpig but better!)

Shopping

Coffee

Skiing

Cooking

CHAPTER 9

GETTING IT RIGHT
FOR A BOY

Throughout my pregnancy with Cameron, Jon and I thought he was going to be another girl.

We misguidedly thought the pattern of the pregnancy was so similar to our first with Eilidh that it must be a girl. It was actually nothing like that first experience. For a start I was the size of a bus, whereas with Eilidh you couldn't tell I was pregnant from behind. I was equally morning sick, but everything else was utterly different. We didn't want to find out the sex of the baby (it was female, obviously), and so it was a huge thrill, but a not insignificant surprise, when he came out very definitely male. To this day, I revel in the genuinely brilliant hand of cards that has dealt me a child of each gender.

But I didn't really know much about boys. I grew up with one sister, and a father who wasn't a blokey, macho type – he seemed quite happy and comfortable in a household of three women, although he still tries to play the multiply hen-pecked card. I spent most of my high-school years at an all-girls local grammar school, although we were very creative about how we socialised with the boys' school. My only other meaningful experiences of males had been boyfriends over the years and a handful of teachers, lecturers and colleagues. So I was thrilled, but distinctly under-informed, and felt more than a bit relieved that Jon would know so much more about bringing up a boy than I did.

But his time for doing so was terribly limited. And so I have worked it out over the years. Not without getting it wrong at times and driving Cameron to despair, I'm sure. His 'tell' is a not-very-subtle eyes rolled to Heaven these days. But most of parenting a boy has been much like parenting a girl. They need love and care and routine and security and occasional excitement or adventures. Until the age of about six or seven, boys need a nurturing, close relationship as much as girls do and while dads are equally able to offer this, it is often mums who are the main care-givers during these early years. After that, though, research suggests that they gradually need to learn how to be, and live, and thrive in the world of men.[8] That's not some type of anti-feminist polemic – their relationship with their mum or other female care-giver remains vital. But the balance shifts, and there are emotional and hormonal arguments to support this.

I haven't been a great reader of self-help books over the years. I have hoped that my instinct would help me make the right decisions about parenting strategies or dilemmas. But I did read a bit about how best to support a boy child because I didn't want to misread the cues Cameron was giving me. Most of what I've done I'd probably have done anyway. I'm not very good at following a script or instructions or recipes, but as he has grown up, I *have* been mindful of taking a step back before reacting to him and thinking about whether it's a boy thing, or a teenage thing, or a Cameron thing.

When he was younger I also tried to make sure he spent time with some of our male friends who had children themselves, so he had some experience of being around dads. But I also deliberately 'targeted' a friend, who didn't have children of his own, although he was step-dad to two older boys. Andrew is one of the most steadfast, principled people I know, and has a great mix of interests in culture, science and sport. I asked him outright if he could act as a sort of

---

8   See Biddulph, S. (2008) *Raising Boys*. New York: Harper Thorsons.

mentor for Cameron, and spend some man-to-boy time with him occasionally.

He agreed, as I knew he would. They got together every few months for a few years, and Andrew was highly generous with his time, and creative in finding science exhibitions, or museums, or Lego festivals to visit. They went to movies (and Eilidh was allowed honorary boy status to see the Hobbit films with them) and played golf. They don't see each other so often now, but I think that's because Cameron did find his way into the 'world of men', with the help and gentle guidance of all our friends – and has also found other ways of being in it just by being himself. And when he and Andrew get together now it's because they genuinely enjoy each other's company – and can have the profound philosophical debates or watch The Matrix Trilogy (which I'm not so good at).

THINGS CAMERON LOVES (AND HE'S DONE THIS ALL BY HIMSELF, UNBIDDEN, IN A HOUSE FULL OF WOMEN...)

Iron Man

1960s, 70s, 80s, 90s music – actually just any music not from this century

Drumming

Swimming

Warhammer

His outdated iPod

Architecture

Robotics and bionics

South Park

Philosophy

Sticky toffee pudding, bread and butter pudding, really just any pudding

Blackadder

Chinese food

Steak (the rarer the better)

Cold weather

Scotland

Maths

Cooking

Skiing

I love that I have a better understanding of a boy's view of the world now. I'd have known nothing about tractors or Transformers or engineering or space-elevator technology without Cameron. I think our round-the-table dinner-time chats would have been less wide-ranging, and my exposure to slightly off-piste YouTube humour distinctly limited. Eilidh would, I suspect, have been much more bothered, and less laid back, about boys. And I think our household might have run the risk of feeling intensely female. I love Cameron's polymath enthusiasms for most subjects you care to name – not necessarily a male-only trait, but so like Jon it often brings me up short. Cameron has occasionally said he feels outnumbered in our family, but as he gets older, I think he is very capably fighting – no, not fighting, but asserting – his male corner. I have no doubt he would have experienced lots of different things had Jon still been with us, but I don't believe he has missed out, or is lacking, because of that.

CHAPTER 10

NEW RELATIONSHIPS

For a long time I had no thoughts about wanting to be in another relationship. Missing Jon was a physical and emotional pain. In the first few years after he died I didn't actually accept that he had gone forever. I had such vivid thoughts and dreams about him, I felt I should be able to touch him and feel the reality of him, because my thoughts of him were so vital and alive. He was constantly with me. And I remembered so many of the funny and happy bits of him, it was hard for a while to believe that he had felt driven by desperation to take his own life. In my dreams, all sorts of scenarios played out where he had somehow faked his death and was alive and living somewhere else. I had not seen his body after he died (advised against it by the undertaker), and so in my state of denial, the possibility of him not being dead became increasingly real for a while. I remembered the firm strength and the feel of his body so clearly, and knew how much he had respected it, that I found it hard to believe he could have done such terrible damage to it.

Time, of course, gradually made that pain less harsh. My dreams about Jon went through phases. After the ones where I thought he was still alive but somewhere else (and always serious and never talking) came the ones where I woke up having just been in the most vivid, everyday situation with him still with us – but knowing as soon as I woke up that he was dead. And eventually, I had dreams where I knew he wasn't alive, but he seemed to be happy, and somewhere good. That was when I went for a walk on Arthur's Seat for the first time since he died. I hadn't deliberately avoided it – you can't live in Edinburgh and not see it all the time. But I hadn't felt like going to it until then. I hiked around some of our favourite areas, and then walked to where I knew he had died. Before that, I couldn't believe that he had left our home on the day he died, and within the space of half an hour arrived there, parked the car, changed out of his suit into walking clothes, climbed the hill, and then fallen to his death. As soon as I stood at the top of the cliff above the new Scottish Parliament building, though, I could see exactly how and where he had walked: less than ten minutes from the car park at Holyrood Palace.

It was a moment of complete revelation – not just of the fact that it had been logistically possible, but that he really was dead. And although that was stark and painful it also felt as if something which had been very stuck for two years had shifted inside me, and a physical weight had been (partly) lifted.

Sometime after that, I began to wake up to the world of relationship potential. Not in a sudden, lightning bolt way which led me to pursue a wild social life seeking out single men – not really my style. But gosh, the games the mind of a young widow plays. Fantasy day dreams about the men I noticed in my everyday life – no *actual* real-life single men at that point, as all my friends were, as I've already said, happily in long-term relationships and so not in a position to introduce me to any conveniently single men. But there was a great choice of children's entertainment personalities (given our life-stage at the time) and even unlikely politicians (I worry for myself in retrospect!) about whom I had surprisingly vivid dreams in those early years.

I also remember an occasion when I was invited to dinner by good friends. They had invited a few other people, including two men who were there by themselves – although not, I think, with the intention of any matchmaking. They were all good people (whom I've met often since then), but the conversations were notably deep and meaningful. So deep and seriously meaningful that halfway through the meal I was tempted to jump on the table and dance with my clothes off to try and shake things up a bit. I didn't. But I did realise afterwards that what was really going on was that I was aching for Jon to be there with me, and I would even have put up with his mischievous, sometimes inappropriate and confrontational style if it meant having a bit of a giggle.

Instead, I dipped my toe into Internet dating a couple of times, albeit a few years apart. The first effort was depressing, the second equally so, but I'd forgotten how bad it made me feel first time round. I know lots of people who have had a great time using Internet dating, and many who have met their life partners through it. I'm not down on Internet dating per se, just for me. Well known as a Luddite in terms of social media (I don't do any of it), I felt the whole process laid me bare. I felt scrutinised (not in a good way), and had one too many scrapes with creepy men. There was the one who had clearly photoshopped his picture and was actually two inches shorter than me (I'm not tall). He talked non-stop through dinner (so much so that the waiter and I got into an eyes-rolled-to-Heaven silent conversation every time he came to the table – 'Is he *really* still talking?'…maybe I should have gone for the waiter…) and was so oblivious to my body language that he was taken aback when I said I didn't think it would be a good idea to meet again.

And then there was the man I never actually met face to face, but from whom I received during a weekend away 16 increasingly irritated voicemails asking why I hadn't got back to his message of two days before – I was very glad that one was in England and had no idea where I lived. And so it went on. Although not for long on either occasion, because what I realised was that my desire to protect the children from a potentially dodgy guy was stronger than my desire to meet a really decent one. The time and effort I needed to give to looking at the dating sites, poring over photos of men who might or might not be what or who they claimed to be, or having to make space in my life for a potentially regular new bit of socialising was time and space of which I had precious little – and I felt my priorities were elsewhere. I loved my life with the children, we had a great social life with friends and family, I worked part time. Dating seemed less important than any of that.

And I was scared – of meeting someone and how to behave, of not meeting someone and being alone forever, of bringing someone into our family of three. Even in the first year after Jon died I wondered how I'd go about meeting someone else, and how to relate to them. I wasn't sure I'd ever been very good at flirting, but by then, I couldn't even remember the definition of the word. What would a man even find attractive? My two small children? My mince-for-brains-hadn't-had-an-intelligent-conversation-for-months? No time to exercise? Rapidly greying hair? I wondered if, when I came upon a man, I'd regress to the stage of a gauche 16-year-old, or just be a highly defensive 35-year-old who had got too used to not being romantic or showing her emotions.

Fifteen years later (grey hair – what was I worried about back then?) the fear is actually no less. In fact it's greater in some ways, because it's now been a very long time without any of that flirty relationship stuff. I had a couple of flings a few years after Jon died. And they were just flings. One was very short lived and not one of my best judgement calls, involving a man I met on a plane to America. What was I thinking?

The other was slightly longer lived, but also not very well judged for all sorts of reasons. Mostly because my head was probably still on another planet, and also because we were utterly ill suited to each other. He was in the military; I was a fairly laissez-faire social worker. His request that I buy very particular boxer shorts from a very particular gentleman's outfitters before he arrived for a visit (I didn't) and his refusal to hold Cameron's hand (very cute and four years old at the time) during a day out were the nails in the coffin. The fact that it satisfied some immediate needs was far from enough to keep it going.

Not long afterwards, I got to know someone who became a good and treasured friend. In many ways bar the most obvious, we were – I suppose – in a relationship. But the commitment to take it to the next level, although something I was prepared to risk, was too difficult for him to make. Over the years, at different times, I was hopeful (fanciful?) that he could let me love him, and might be able to do the same in return. I hoped we could take a risk at making each other happy.

And so it went on until the beginning of this year. Eventually I recognised that I needed to be clear, once and for all, about the prospects for our relationship which had only ever actually been a friendship. I was pouring a lot of emotional energy into it, for lack of anything more like a proper partnership, and was blocking the chance of opening myself up to meeting someone else. He gently but resolutely held to his no-commitment stance, although he would have been happy to continue as we were. I, on the other hand, knew I had to stop seeing him, even though it went against so many of my instincts.

The loss I felt having made that decision was a lot to do with why I started writing this story when I did. These ideas had been in my head for 15 years. I knew that if I was to feel liberated enough to get on with whatever comes next in my life, not only did I have to end that relationship, which had never actually begun, but also to put all of this story into writing.

I don't regret any of what I've done and not done about relationships. At every turn, it has been about Eilidh and Cameron. When they were much younger, I wanted to meet someone mostly so that we could be an ordinary family, so they could have a dad in their lives. I liked the idea of someone being there for me, but in my head it was mostly for them – probably not a good basis for a relationship, so I'm quite relieved it never worked out. And I was filled with doubts about how we might blend our families if he (the hypothetical he) had children (clearly possible because lots of people do it), how we would share the parenting roles and responsibilities (ditto), where we would live (ditto), whose parents we'd spend Christmas with (ditto). You can see where this is going: with hindsight, I wasn't ready to meet anyone, even if there had been a way of it happening naturally. My focus was the children, and I don't think I was ready or able to make space for another significant emotional attachment in my life.

From this distance, I realise that I was also building defences around myself. Over the years, my feelings about Jon shifted between grief and longing, to some bad memories of when things were difficult, to flashes of the brilliant and funny person he was. For a long time this was muddled and relentless and exhausting. And for a long time, but in a vague and subliminal way, it made me doubt my sense of myself. Memories of the difficult times left me feeling bad about myself, questioning myself and leaving my confidence at rock bottom. I remember thinking back to the person I'd been before meeting him, and I didn't recognise her, or the me I became with him.

It took a long time after he died for me to re-identify myself. I never got that original person back, because I'd become a mother by then, and then lost Jon, but I am now me, at least – a new version. On the way to rediscovering me, I was probably not in the best place to get into a new relationship, and maybe at a subconscious level I recognised that fact. Perhaps that was what stopped me making a more concerted effort to meet someone. And maybe my memory of the difficult times – mostly a product of Jon's mental health issues I now understand, but still hard to live with – have made me wary of trusting someone again.

On top of which, I'm quite good at being by myself. Even before Jon died I didn't need to be constantly with him or surrounded by people to feel secure or good or happy. I enjoyed all of that but I liked my own company, too, and I still do. I'm good at filling my time, by myself or with friends. I've been running our family life for 15 years, and I'm quite good at it. A friend and I – she has also raised her child by herself – sometimes wonder if we appear too capable and independent, and perhaps we'd be more likely to meet someone if we played damsels in distress sometimes.

So I have this dilemma: I'm lonely. Not like elderly or single people who have few others in their lives, not like the loneliness some feel inside a difficult relationship or marriage (I had a brief experience of that), but a deep loneliness in my core, which has nothing to do with lacking friends or family or interests or a sense of purpose. I have all of those. But I have a space in my heart and soul which I would love to be filled by someone alongside whom I could live a life, and in my imagination, fill the same sort of space for them. And yet at the same time, I'm getting on with leading an independent, full and busy life. Until now, I've felt that ne'er the twain could meet, but in the past few months, as I've been writing this, and having made the decision to clear my emotional decks, I feel there might be a way, and I feel more open to it than I could have been in the past. And now, it's about the possibility of meeting someone for me, and not a dad for my children.

CHAPTER 11

A WORD ABOUT DREAMS

I am not a dream expert and don't know anything about dream analysis. But I do believe that the dreams I had, and occasionally still have, about Jon have been part of my mourning for him.

As I said in the previous chapter, there did seem to be a pattern in the early years (which seems to be common in bereaved people) whereby my dreams initially had quite grim and bleak images where Jon was troubled or sad or somehow inaccessible to me. Sometimes I would have vivid dreams about our old life having just carried on, where he was still part of our everyday family life. And after those, I had more dreams where I seemed to understand that he was no longer alive, but wasn't in pain or suffering in any way.

I have always thought that my sleeping brain processed the emotions which I couldn't let out in everyday life. My fairly buttoned-up, keep-very-busy path through grief allowed me to keep relatively on top of my responsibilities to the children, in a way that 'wailing and gnashing of teeth' would not. But my feelings were all still there, and dreaming time was obviously where they could play out. And I often woke from the most vivid dreams back in the deepest of grief, as I realised that Jon wasn't in fact still here. Even as I was dreaming, there was a small conscious part of me that knew he was dead, and so although the dreaming might have been about him being here with us, those images went hand in hand with the pain of knowing he wasn't really.

Probably a bit like the process of moving through the stages of bereavement, there was a general pattern to the dreams I had, which were helping me to do some grief work while I had some uninterrupted space to do it. But as time has passed, there have been some dream-time surprises which threw up incredibly vivid images at times I would never have expected. Even a long while after my first trip to Arthur's Seat, when I really thought I'd rationalised Jon's death, I had a very powerful dream that he *had* actually faked his death. We met again some years later, and just started our relationship all over again, and he got to know the children at the stage they were at. And it seemed so good and so right that when I woke and realised it wasn't real it came like a physical blow.

There have continued to be a whole assortment of dreams over the last few years, albeit much less frequently. Mostly, they feature Jon in perfectly ordinary scenarios with me, or I meet someone in a certain situation, but it's actually him. Nothing earth shattering any more, but I always tend to wake with an 'Oh that was him' realisation. Apart from the dreams from which I would wake convinced that he was still alive, which were too painful to be helpful, all the others have always felt comforting and somehow reassuring – nothing by which to be scared or troubled. And I have been grateful that my subconscious has continued to do a lot of the hard work of moving me on, trying to make sense of what happened.

CHAPTER 12

ACCEPTANCE

Oh my: there is a lot to accept. When 'acceptance' is bandied about as a concept following a bereavement (or any traumatic life event) it is perhaps acceptance of the event itself which is sought. For me, as I've said, that took a while, mainly because of the circumstances of Jon's death and my fantasies that it might have been faked. I suppose the rational part of me always accepted it, after the first brief period of shock, but it took a lot longer to disprove those fantasies and allow reality to really bite. It wasn't as if I hadn't been 'bitten' already, but acceptance is not a pain-free process. As soon as I went to Arthur's Seat and saw how and where Jon took his life, I did feel part of the weight of his loss lifting with that acceptance – the doubt part, anyway. But it also made his loss completely real. And with that came a different level of pain, which took more time to pass. Acceptance demands absolute honesty when all of the defences created by denial fall away, and that will always be painful at first, even if the end point is one of openness and optimism.

Grasping the reality of Jon's death was only the first of a number of things I have accepted over the years, but there are others which I know I am still struggling to achieve. I don't know if this is specific to losing someone to suicide, but I suspect not. I'm sure there are layers of acceptance to be climbed through after any loss, and some of these will prove more challenging than others. I still look at mothers with tiny babies, and it takes me right back to when Jon died. My automatic assumption, even now, is to wonder if the dad is still around, or if he may have chosen to take his own life. It's a fleeting thought, and it's not normal, I know. But it was my experience, my normal, and so the question mark is hard-wired now. I'm still waiting to find some kind of acceptance of that.

I have been slightly more successful with the screaming inside my head. This has gone on for years in different ways, triggered by different things – initially by the appalling reality of Jon's death, and, later, by my perception of the injustice of it, most often when we saw 'proper' families together. Other people who haven't been through something similar cannot really get it. All of them sympathise, some genuinely empathise – and those who do are well-cherished friends. But they don't inhabit my experience, or understand it in the way that it has inhabited my every fibre and pore. And they don't hear the screaming inside my head. But – and this is a but that I have recognised only after many years – nor would I *want* them to do either of those things. As I said earlier I would not wish such experiences on anyone.

And maybe this is where acceptance is found, at least for this bit of my life: that this has been my experience, not anyone else's, and it is unfair and unrealistic to think they could imagine what it has really been like. I have also realised that the screaming inside my head can, and needs to, stop. That is why I'm writing this at this time in my life. I just passed my 50th birthday milestone, and the children are approaching new and exciting stages in their life.

I realise that I need to let go of the frustration I've sometimes experienced at what feels like other people's lack of understanding or perception. Because that was not their fault. None of us can or should be expected to emotionally inhabit the multiple life experiences of everyone we know. Empathy and consideration are more than good enough. The frustration I have felt over the years has had the potential to hold me back from all the things I want to do now, and the person I want to be in future. So I am trying to let it go. Acceptance, or letting go? I think they are interconnected.

And acceptance has also happened imperceptibly and unbidden at the transitions between different points on my path through mourning, especially with regard to socialising. The earliest months, when any social effort felt like wading through treacle or looking through a fuzzy lens, transitioned to the next phase – being able to put on a brave face and make a better pretence of having a good time. And that phase eventually evolved into *genuinely* having a good time. Each stage added a new layer of acceptance. I'm not sure the task will ever be fully completed. But it is completed enough to feel good, and honest and optimistic.

Letting go and acceptance may be synonymous with each other, but they are also inextricably linked to the benefits of time passing. Speaking from the high vantage point of 15 years passing, I do believe that 'time heals' a loss, but it's like a scar forming rather than recovering from flu. It gets better, but it doesn't ever fully disappear. And if someone tried to tell me at three, or five, or even eight years along the path that time was healing me, I'd have been tempted to tell them where to go. Today though, I feel inside, and therefore accept, that it is true. The passage of time for me with Eilidh and Cameron has allowed them to grow up, and become my allies as much as the children I need to protect. In and of itself, this has made the tasks of acceptance so much easier.

And I can't stress enough how important it is to be kind to yourself, to cut yourself some slack. I keep coming back to it, but especially when there is no other adult at home to tell you, it is OK – and indeed essential – that you tell yourself. What I've learned about acceptance is that it's unlikely to happen if stress, self-criticism or frustration are ever-present. They all complicate and blur the situation, and create barriers to being able to move forward. Don't, for example, underestimate the effort it takes to keep motivated about every aspect of your life – caring for the children, maintaining friendships, trying something new, keeping up with your fitness or gym plans, applying for a new job. Little children are fabulous joy bringers but not renowned for their sensitivity to others' feelings. When Eilidh and Cameron were younger there was *never* a 'How was your day?/That must have been tough/Can I give you a hand?/Don't speak to your mother like that' at the end of the day. And that, for a long time, only served to reinforce Jon's absence, and block the elusive acceptance.

I'm not sure if I could have done anything to change that, or hasten the process. I never wanted to get into a situation of nagging the children or guilt-tripping them into perceiving my needs – they were little children, by their natures fairly self-absorbed, and already dealing with more emotional baggage than they should have been. I also wasn't going to let go of any of the things I fitted into our lives – all of it was important in different ways. So I suppose what I accepted back then was that those were all my choices, and that by making them I was probably prolonging the acceptance of Jon's loss and all its implications.

What I should have done was stop beating myself up about everything. I set very high expectations of myself, in my own right but also for the children. Somehow, being a single parent made me more determined that I had to be the perfect parent, and I thought that if they weren't polite, or handing in brilliant homework ('all their own work' but with hours of parental involvement), not wearing polished shoes every week, or not going to a wholesome range of sports and activities then it would reflect really badly on me, and me alone. I actually believed that in every fibre of my being until I had my breakdown. And even afterwards, I learned ridiculously slowly how mistaken I was. No one was judging me except me. I know now (sorry for blowing my own trumpet) that the people who knew me best thought I was doing a good job. And I can look back and see they were right.

But objectivity is almost impossible without another supportive caring adult alongside you to offer it. When you are at the lowest ebbs of grief, or just exhausted by everything that it takes to hold your life together, it is hard to take a step back and congratulate yourself on how well you are doing. But try and make time to do it, and to objectively look at what you have achieved in the past day, or week or month. Whatever it was, be proud of yourself, and if you feel like sharing it with someone else, do. From where I stand now, I wish I had been kinder and more back-patting to myself, and been able to honestly appraise what I was achieving every day. I think I would have been much more able to reach points of acceptance more quickly if I had done so.

CHAPTER 13

WHEN IS IT OK TO USE BEREAVEMENT AS AN EXCUSE?

This isn't really a serious question. I mean, it is, but that's not why it's here.

The serious answer would be very long, and would go into lots of detail about whether or not someone ends up being defined by their loss, and can't move on with a new phase of their life. That is serious and upsetting, and if you're reading this and feel that you might be falling into that place, please think about asking someone for some help or support.

My real intention was to squeeze in a silly anecdote which still makes us giggle (and have the good grace to feel slightly ashamed) many years later. We were camping for a few nights at a beautiful campsite in Dumfries and Galloway, overlooking the Solway Firth. We were using a huge tent (a canvas palace) borrowed from a friend instead of our own more basic version, and were anticipating a great holiday. Cameron was already making friends at the park. Eilidh was deep in one of her books. All was boding well.

Our neighbour in the next-door tent was there with her teenaged daughter. Even as we were pitching the tent, she had come up and started to chat – very friendly. They were there for a few days break too. But within a short time, having already heard a large portion of her life story whenever I emerged from our tent, I realised I had to staunch the flow of her conversation or we wouldn't get a moment's peace. So I told her that this was in fact the first camping holiday we'd had by ourselves since my husband died (not actually a lie, as all previous camping trips had involved other people) and I would be really grateful it if she could respect our privacy as I wasn't sure how the children were going to manage. She was appropriately sympathetic, and asked when my husband passed away. Fully aware that the children were in the tent, no doubt stuffing their fists in their mouths to stifle their giggles, I said in a slightly wavery voice 'Oh...not so very long ago' (it was nine years). I then retreated to the tent where we (hopefully soundlessly) collapsed in hysterics. 'Oh, not so very long ago' has become something of a family catchphrase. And bless her, our talkative neighbour did respect our privacy and we had a gorgeous holiday.

Eilidh was always the doyenne of using bereavement as an excuse. For many years, from about the age of four to seven, when she was naughty or I needed to tell her off for something, she would often tremble her bottom lip and say, 'I miss my Daddy'. What mother could carry on hard-heartedly and stick to her boundary-setting guns? Eilidh usually ended up with a cuddle and a reassuring chat, and a quick message of 'But it doesn't mean you can do naughty things.' Years later, she admitted it was a deliberate strategy to get off lightly. She wasn't daft. Down the years I can still imagine her six-year-old self doing a fist pump and saying 'Gotcha!' as she escaped from yet another reprimand.

CHAPTER 14

THE GOOD BITS

Over the years, there have always been times when I've felt more as if I've been surviving – just – rather than thriving, but those times have become fewer and further between, and are now very rare. My relentless need to keep busy and make plans, which was an unconscious survival strategy in the early years, has become calmer, but I'm still, by nature, a busy person, and there are rarely any unplanned times on the calendar. But that's fine, and I can ease the pace if I ever feel it's going too fast. I've become much better at recognising my own limits, and know when to ask for help, or to take a step back and reflect on things. At the start of this year of turning 50 I knew that I needed to clear some of my decks, and work out where I was heading next, and as I sit here today, I feel more comfortable in my own skin than ever before.

Even when the earliest years were full of pain and fear and uncertainty, there were always also lots of wonderful times, because the children were a constant source of joy and laughter and amazement. All of that great stuff just ran alongside the harder stuff, so life wasn't either good or bad, joyful or painful; it was all of it together, but in different proportions at different times.

We have a great life, with a Jon-sized gap. Over the years, the gap hasn't changed in size, but the impact it makes on our lives has diminished. I've done lots of the things with Eilidh and Cameron that Jon and I would have done, because I'd have done them anyway –

hill walking, sharing our love of books, exploring foreign countries, eating increasingly spicy curries, spending time with our old friends and their growing families...weekends and holidays and Hogmanay celebrations. But not as much camping as we would have done with him, no scuba diving and definitely no DIY bike maintenance. I've never become any less impatient with the computer when it goes wrong, and my woodwork skills are fairly basic.

But the children have grown up in a home full of unconditional love and fun, and I don't feel that they have been neglected because of the things I haven't done with them. I've done the things that I could share with and pass on to them. We've always had friends in and out of our home, sharing playtime when they were little, and meals and weekends. When Eilidh and Cameron were young I loved doing creative stuff together – tie-dyeing, autumn leaf pictures, floor-sized painting sessions, hours of Play-Doh cafes or huge cardboard box creations. And there were days spent at old castles, or at the beach, or making obstacle courses around the house, playing hide-and-seek before bath time, having movie nights snuggled together on the sofa. I couldn't babysit at night for friends, but we often had friends' children around during the days instead, and after the first couple of years when that used to make me teeter on the verge of losing control, it just became part of family life – as it is for most families. And I suppose that's where 'moving on' might be found. Not that the Jon-sized gap has ever disappeared, but we have made a life for the three of us which is our everyday, very like many other families' everyday – and good. Great, even.

And the other good bits? Although single parenting for non-widowed people is obviously slightly different, as the mother/father may still have some input, the benefits of single parenting are actually multiple – not having to consult on any major decisions such as holiday plans, decorating, eating sundried tomatoes (which Jon regarded as wasteful, extortionately priced food of the devil). No tension over how to parent the children, over life decisions, or who's going to change the lightbulb, or who does more housework/cooking/shopping. No debates about where to send the children to school – he wanted them to have private education, I didn't.

I know from watching coupled friends over the years that all of those big and little issues can lead to big and little tensions, and we've never had to deal with any of those. Having to make all the decisions alone can become exhausting or tedious or boring at times, but it has also been liberating and empowering. Anything that needs to be done in the house has to be done or organised by me, but that just means I do some slightly incompetent power drilling myself to put up a shelf, or if it's too big or heavy, I'll pay someone competent to do it instead. And if something doesn't work out as expected, I can only blame myself, and can't fall into some relationships' trap of guilt-tripping or recriminations.

Although some friends' relationships have been through ups and downs, I also know that many of our friends and relations found Jon's suicide brought perspective, in a way none of us could have predicted. Over the years many people have said it restored their sense of balance when they were feeling close to the edge of something, and helped them realise nothing was so bad it couldn't be dealt with. Something along the lines of being thankful for small mercies, or making the most of life because it isn't a rehearsal. And there have also been revelations by a number of people I know well who experienced the death by suicide of someone close to them in the distant past but had not felt comfortable discussing it. They said that the openness with which we have faced Jon's death as a family helped them to revisit their own memories in a more open way. So it hasn't just been us who have found some light after Jon's death.

Would I have made different choices about my career had Jon still been alive? Yes, I'm sure I would. Do I regret that? Not really, because I've loved the work I've been able to do, and I would not otherwise have had the same relationships, or time, with Eilidh and Cameron. Would we still be living in the same house? Probably not, but nor would we have had friendships which are now 20 years old with our friends and neighbours here. There would have been different friends, but I love the community we live in and the feeling of being surrounded by good people we have known for a long time.

And would I prefer the children to have had their dad as part of their lives? Yes, of course. Jon was so full of energy and enthusiasm for so many different things, active and thoughtful, daft and serious. Having to be two parents at once for 15 years hasn't been easy. In so many situations, it would have been lovely to have been able to 'divide and conquer' like two-parent families can – on holidays or at weekends, or even helping with homework or any of the other multitude of everyday things with which they've needed support. I wish the children could have had some one-to-one time with both of us, and been able to do more of the things they loved best. Instead, our time together has usually involved a degree of compromise, trying to find a mixture of activities that keep both Eilidh and Cameron (who have fairly disparate likes, dislikes and personalities) happy and occupied. Mostly, I think it has worked out OK, and learning the art of compromise and negotiation is a helpful life lesson to tick off early on. But yes, honestly, it would all have been much easier had I not been doing it alone. The problem, as I said earlier, is that if Jon were still here, he would be dealing with his demons, and our lives would all have been affected. I am grateful that Cameron and Eilidh have not had to live with that.

Many of the good bits are bittersweet. Everything the children have achieved at every age, actually. Cameron's first words, both being potty trained, first days at school, good school reports, dance shows, swimming competitions, first drawings, all their drawings, climbing their first Munro, learning to ski, riding a bike without stabilisers, getting the bus into town by themselves, going to high school, making me laugh, making me think, hearing them laugh together or being kind to someone else. Every single amazing thing they've ever done, Jon has missed. And I feel the sadness of that for him, and for the children, every time. But we often bring other loved people along instead – to the dance shows or prize-givings, and all of the Munros we've climbed together have been with my parents.

And I treasure all the memories of all those things extra specially because there isn't another parent to share that privilege. While lots of elements in both of them remind me strongly of their dad – Eilidh's spirit of adventure and courageous approach, Cameron's energy and enthusiasm for new ideas and discoveries – so much of them is just about them being themselves. Every new thing they try or achieve, I have felt responsible for giving them the confidence to tackle, and I don't mean that in a self-congratulatory way. It's just what all parents should do, but as a single parent, letting them take the risks falls on your shoulders alone – but then so does the thrill of them succeeding.

JOYFUL MOMENTS (THEY'RE THERE IF YOU LOOK)

Being at the top of any hill, big or small

Overhearing Eilidh and Cam belly-laughing at something together

Double rainbows, or actually, any rainbows

Hogmanay – watching all our friends and children dancing Strip the Willow

The 2m² AstroTurf garden in front of a nearby house

Driving to the Cairngorms, windows down, playing 'Born to be Wild' full tilt

The incredible berries on the rowan trees this autumn

Watching a seagull paddle-dancing on grass with both feet to bring up worms

The surprise party my girlfriends threw for my 50th

That delicious polenta and pistachio cake

Strictly Come Dancing (sparkle and fizz are good for the soul)

Beautiful things made by talented people

When the children tell me something brilliant or clever or funny

When the agapanthus blossoms in the summer

The first mouthful of any wine shared with friends

Kitchen dancing

Michelle Obama doing carpool karaoke with James Corden

CHAPTER 15

WHAT DOESN'T KILL YOU

Well, it didn't kill me, but whether I'm stronger is really unanswerable. I've lived the last 15 years instinctively, most of the time trying to do what I thought was best for the children, but sometimes probably getting that wrong, like all parents do. Sometimes it has felt like lurching from one decision, one plan, one crisis, to another. But we're all still in one piece, if maybe a bit ragged around the edges. And for the most part, life has been good, and not infrequently great. I don't know what person I would have been had Jon still been here. I suspect there would have been other tests of my resilience, and I may have been found wanting.

When Jon died I received cards from many friends and relatives. Many had clearly taken a lot of time, and put a lot of thought into writing insightful letters, with memories and perceptions of Jon. One has stayed with me for different reasons. It was from an ex-girlfriend of Jon's, who I didn't really know well. Among the recollections and memories, she also said she believed that no matter how desperate Jon felt, he would not have made the decision to take his own life if he didn't believe I could cope with the aftermath.

Maybe she was right. Resilience is a fluid concept – people are not just completely resilient, or completely vulnerable. They can be more or less resilient at different times and under different provocations. But the end point is the important one – whether or not you 'get through' whatever challenge you face, not necessarily whether you do it with style, grace or dignity. And having survived thus far, I suppose I can accept that, on balance, resilience wins out.

The way I grieved and subsequently lived my life was partly choice – what I thought was best for the children – and partly just because of the person I am. Could I have avoided the walls tumbling seven years ago (and the mortar being a bit more eroded this year) if I'd let a bit more of my grief out in manageable chunks over the years? Should I have expressed my sadness and loneliness more explicitly, and asked for help more often? These are rhetorical questions which I can't actually answer. I've done what I've done and lived how I've lived. And the fact that we're here, with lots of brilliant things going on in our lives, makes me think the peaks and troughs between there and here were part of what led us to this point. There may have been a different route – as the re-working of bereavement theories over the decades showed – but this was my route.

It's another of the 'what if' questions that I've asked myself over the past 15 years, or that other people have asked. Eilidh has often wanted to know what I think life would have been like had Jon still been here. When she was younger, I'm sure this was about wanting to imagine a lovely picture of our family with two parents, and at that stage, I didn't disillusion her. But as she's got older, I've been increasingly honest with her. This is one of those concepts that genuinely plays with my head: I can make the leap to Jon still being alive, but then the reality of what he would have been like, as a father to teenagers and a partner to me, flies off into fantastical territory. Because if he *were* here, and by some miracle had resisted his suicidal instinct, he would still have been a complex, troubled person, struggling with his mental health. His resistance to seeking professional help for this would not have disappeared. He would have been unpredictable, and swung between anger and depression, but also been a great dad. I would have tried to support him through it all, while trying to protect the children from the worst effects. From my personal and professional experiences of seeing families who have had to deal with those kinds of situations, I can at least be relieved that we never had to cope with that. Our loss of Jon has been and always will be painful, but to face what could have been a daily reality of helping him through the unforgiving and traumatic experience of chronic mental ill health would have undoubtedly taken a different kind of toll on all of us.

I may not have got it right all the time, but at least I've been able to do it my way, and therefore only have myself to blame if something hasn't worked out. If a measure of 'surviving' or being made stronger is needed, I suppose I default to the fact that Eilidh and Cameron, at this point in their lives, seem to be happy and well-balanced young adults. I couldn't wish for anything else. They are (usually) kind, thoughtful, perceptive and funny. They are doing well at school, have good friends, and have found interests that fire them up. They have wobbly times – maybe to do with being teenagers, maybe to do with the fact their dad took his own life – but they learn something from these each time and the next occurrence seems slightly less scary to deal with.

One of my greatest regrets is that Jon wasn't ever part of our life as a family with two children. He knew the crazy disorientation of life with a toddler and a baby on the way, and had two brief weeks with both children. For us, and I suspect for many new parents, it was a time of sudden imposition of incompetence – sleep deprivation, incessant breastfeeding, colic, controlled crying and not having the answer to most baby-related situations. We did have a lot of fun, too, though – holidays in Scotland and France, hill walks, bike rides and lots of time with our families.

But he has missed so much. Our children are amazing young people, and he knew nothing of all their interests and skills and loves and hates, their opinions and beliefs. He shared none of our holidays, never helped them with any of their homework. Part of my subconscious still can't help thinking 'If only he'd known what our family life would be like' – but there's that mind-knotting thought process again. It's a game that I really have to stop playing.

TODAY THE BALANCE FEELS RIGHT

Most of the time, most days, I love our life. I relish the things we do together, the things I do by myself and with friends. I take genuine pleasure from them all. And as the years have gone by, this sense of rightness with the world has increased proportionately to the sense of loss and grief and sadness. That will never leave me and I will feel it for myself, but especially for Eilidh and Cameron, for the rest of my life. But those feelings have found a place which is bearable. More than bearable – just part of life. Writing this has really made clear how great a sense of perspective I have now compared to various points in the past. That's not to say I will never lose that sense of perspective in future – I think it's highly likely. But I know that when I do, I will be able to deal with it, and come out the other side.

My measure? Probably the fact that I'm writing this now. I think it marks my need to make these thoughts and feelings external, processing all of this and finding a place to keep it safe, somewhere in my head or heart, but where it isn't at the forefront any longer. And maybe this is a means to finding the next direction, a new direction. We haven't been on the two-parent conveyor belt for the past 15 years, but I finally feel that the one-parent version is actually OK.

My friend Kate phoned a week or so after we had all had dinner together earlier this year when she was visiting Edinburgh. Eilidh, Cameron and I had been walking ahead of her and her daughter as we headed back to their apartment. Kate knew Jon – she'd seen us through buying our first home together, getting married, having both babies. She liked and respected him, and has felt his loss greatly over the years. But she told me that when she looked at us walking together arm in arm she realised there was nothing missing, that we did not look like a family with a gap. She told me, 'You have made your family complete.' I think Jon would have been glad about that.

PLEASE REMEMBER

For anyone who is going through something like we experienced, it does get better. Please ask for help. You are not alone. Speak to friends or family, or someone at the end of a helpline (see the numbers in the Appendix).

For anyone who thinks someone they care about is going through something similar to us, please be the person they can talk to. Pre-empt them asking…talk to them first. Nothing you say or do will be the wrong thing if it is done with love and concern.

For anyone who might feel that suicide is the only way out, please ask someone for help – anyone you think you can trust, your GP, someone at the end of a helpline (see the numbers in the Appendix). You are cared about and valued and you would be missed. Please.

A MAN CALLED JON

By Eilidh[9]

I am like my dad. Even as a baby I was like him – both feisty, scrawny and bald; reminiscent of Benjamin Button. Thankfully my hair grew, and the similarities we have shared relate more to our passions and personalities – a mutual spirit for adventure, determination and pushing the boundaries. A love of the mountains, the sea, great heights (preferably from which to skydive, although as safely as possible to keep mum happy) and the vast expanse of books in the world. From eating toast together before he headed to work and falling asleep on the back of his bike as a toddler, to now being at one with the water and waves, or in a harness atop a high precipice, our shared genetics are laid bare.

I would not go so far as to identify as an adrenaline junky (far from it) but my dad did tend that way in his younger years. Even as a young boy he was always experimenting with new projects. Good with his hands, he designed tents and dens, built endless kites and other forms of his own personal entertainment; culminating in his most glorious construction – a go-kart. He promptly test-drove it vertically down Arthur's Seat and plunged it into the duck pond. His pursuits developed at university and led him to push further limits. He joined the scuba club and built on his mountaineering and

---

9   Story submitted as part of Eilidh's Advanced Higher English portfolio.

climbing talents. His friendships with the like-minded soulmates he met through these pursuits led to various other ill-thought-out, drink-fuelled actions – attaching a sofa to the back of someone's car and driving fast through a field with several people on it was perhaps not his finest moment. Nor were the decisions to ski (in broad daylight) completely stark naked or to dive (head first) off a boat in the dark, having been told explicitly not to. Nevertheless, if it weren't for his audacious ways, I may never have been here to take on his characteristics. Had it not been for a fateful night where he managed to wedge an ice axe in the bridge of his nose while practising climbing on a door-jam, he and my mother may not have bonded as they managed to, after his panicked search for someone sober enough to drive him to hospital. He mellowed with age but the tendency to thrill-seek remained a trait common to both of us.

While I am my father's daughter, the genes I have from my mum provide a balance to those from my edge-living dad. I may not take things to quite the extremes that he did in the past but I do have that daredevil inside me who seeks the rush of taking a risk – albeit a calculated one in my case. I was always a curious little girl – taking pleasure from clambering on crags and rocks as a child but also in safer ways like rifling through people's handbags when they weren't looking. At an age where I couldn't take risks, I made mischief – flooding the toilets at school, stealing sweets from shops and squeezing very hard on one of the baby chicks we had in nursery; purely because I wanted to see what would happen in each case. And yes, my family did think I was a small psychopath for a while.

Now that I have reached young adulthood I am more aware of our likeness than ever. I share his love for the sea and being on the water – surfing, kayaking and rowing. One day I hope to follow in his footsteps and take up scuba diving: he would be the best teacher. There is nothing so powerful as being rendered completely helpless by one huge wave. The adrenaline that comes from knowing that you are at risk by doing something you love is unparalleled and electrifies every fibre of your being. When I climb a mountain, and reach its peak, the wind blowing through my hair and the bite of the cold against my skin remind me of how high I have climbed. Nothing compares to that sweaty exhaustion that engulfs me as I stand and look down; seeing more of the world than many people could imagine. I know that this is what my dad and I have shared; those sensations and rushes of adrenaline that some people will never experience. It is the buzz when you catch a wave and ride it successfully that drives me to look for the next, bigger one; and the joy that overcomes me when I see what the landscape of Scotland looks like to a bird which pushes me to reach for the next summit. I yearn to discover more and challenge myself to push the boundaries further, just like my dad.

He always liked to push the boundaries. Pushing them as far as they could stretch, before springing back into place with the twang of an elastic band. Sometimes things get pushed too far, and suddenly there is no recoil of elastic as everything goes back to normal. Because sometimes we do things that seem like a good idea at the time, and normal will not be the same again. We take mental risks as well as physical. Human nature dictates that there will always be those who push too hard and who will push the elastic to breaking point. Sometimes a man will see things he wishes to forget and feel things he cannot explain. A man may take a risk that there is no coming back from.

My dad liked to take risks. One morning in August 2001, he staked everything on one final act.

* * * * *

A man called Jon climbed the crags at Arthur Seat, one morning in August 2001. It was a weekday, quiet, when most people were at work or following the normal morning routine. Later that day a policeman knocked on the door of a house and told a woman that Jon would not be coming home.

For a long time, I felt betrayed. I felt betrayed by a person who was no longer there. Betrayed by a person I could no longer blame.

All my life I had been told that my dad loved me, unconditionally and always. Yet, he left me. He walked out of the front door one morning and said goodbye to me, knowing that he was never coming back. I felt that he had abandoned me.

I still feel betrayed, but not by him. I feel betrayed by life. My dad was amazing. He was witty and smart, brave and adventurous. I no longer feel abandoned, I feel sad. I am sad because he was scared and hurting. He did what he felt was his only option and I believe that what he did took incredible amounts of courage. And I am sad because he is not a part of my life. He wasn't there for the first day of school, the first time I rode a bike or the first time I stood up on a surfboard. He won't be there when I finish high school or start university this year. He won't interrogate my boyfriends or defend my honour. He won't be there to walk me down the aisle on my wedding day. I will never see him hold his first grandchild with a tear in his eye. For all these reasons, I wish life could have been different. In spite of this, I am glad he was my father.

I am like my dad in countless ways, but I will not be like the man called Jon.

USEFUL INFORMATION

HELPFUL ORGANISATIONS
1. For adults ·

Cruse Bereavement Care
www.crusescotland.org.uk
support@crusescotland.org.uk
0845 600 2227 in Scotland or
www.cruse.org.uk
helpline@cruse.org.uk
0844 477 9400 in England, Wales and Northern Ireland

Cruse is the longest established national bereavement support organisation, set up in 1959. They offer 'an impartial ear with no agenda', via direct, personal support sessions or phone consultations. All forms of support are offered free of charge.

Samaritans
www.samaritans.org
jo@samaritans.org
Phone (free): 116 123 from anywhere in the UK

The Samaritans are known nationally for their support for people who are at risk of taking their own lives, but also offer help and support to anyone in need and not just those who are suicidal. Their website states that 'it doesn't matter who you are, how you feel, or what has happened. If you feel that things are getting to you, get in touch. We know a lot about what can help you through tough times. We can help you explore your options, understand your problems better, or just be there to listen.' Like Cruse, the support offered by Samaritans is free of charge at the point of use.

Your local NHS website
This will show you lists of accredited counselling and other support services. Or you can ask your GP directly for their advice, or a referral, in this regard.

CALM – The Campaign Against Living Miserably
www.thecalmzone.net

CALM is an award-winning charity dedicated to preventing male suicide, whose increasingly high profile is gaining them and their work much welcome publicity.

Childhood Bereavement Network
www.childhoodbereavementnetwork.org.uk

A national (UK) hub for organisations working with bereaved children, and who also offer signposting for families, professionals or the public to sources of bereavement support in their local area.

Support after Suicide Partnership
http:\\supportaftersuicide.org.uk

A national (UK) hub for organisations and individuals who work to support people bereaved or affected by suicide. The website offers advice about practical and emotional support issues, both for those affected and those trying to support them. It also offers signposting to local sources of help and advice.

2. For children (our own experience)

Richmond's Hope
227 Niddrie Mains Road
Edinburgh EH16 4PA
www.richmondshope.org.uk
info@richmondshope.org.uk
0131 661 6818 (City of Edinburgh and Midlothian) or
0141 230 6123 (Glasgow, based in Govan)

Richmond's Hope is our local bereavement support organisation, and we have been supported by them for the past four years. The charity was set up in 2003, and has grown in expertise and scope since then. They support children aged between four and 18 years who have been bereaved (by natural death, suicide or murder) with sensitivity and compassion. Their mission statement is that 'we believe we can make a difference in the lives of people who have been bereaved by supporting them through their grief using therapeutic play providing a safe haven for them to work out their feelings'.

You can self-refer, by phone or email. After a phone discussion to take basic details, you will have a face-to-face meeting to find out if it would help your child to come to Richmond's. They say that 'it is important that children want to come to the project and we will do everything we can to make them feel welcome'. If this is the case, you will be offered one-to-one sessions (40 minutes per week) for up to 12 weeks.

In addition to these individual sessions, Richmond's Hope provide family support in the form of away days or family sessions; a fortnightly teenager's support group; a lending library; and telephone support and advice.

There are outreach playrooms now in Dalkeith and North West Edinburgh in addition to the original base in Niddrie.

Winston's Wish
17 Royal Crescent
Cheltenham
GL50 3DA
www.winstonswish.org
info@winstonswish.org
08088 020021 (freephone helpline)

Winston's Wish was the first bereavement support organisation we made touch with, nine years ago. They were established in 1992 and were the first national children's bereavement organisation in Britain. On their website they say 'at a time when you are experiencing your own grief at the death of a partner, child, family member or friend, it can seem overwhelming to offer support to your child or children. Winston's Wish can support you and your family through this process.'

As with Richmond's, we found their expert support to be kind, wise and gentle – and it has given us strategies to cope as more time has passed. They provide direct support and advice to families and children, in person and through their helpline and various online forums or personal email routes. They offer a variety of direct interventions – support groups, and day or weekend groups. They can provide advice for teachers on how best to support bereaved children in their class, and have resources and publications for sale, for schools and for families. They also offer monthly drop-in support sessions.

Please check online or with your GP for supportive agencies near to where you live.

BEYOND BEREAVEMENT COUNSELLING

I found both of the following approaches helpful at different times in the past fifteen years. If you think you might need more than some general counselling to help you get through the most difficult times, these might be worth considering. You can read about both online: I found information from the Royal College of Psychiatrists, MIND, BeMindful.co.uk and the NHS, all of whose advice has its basis in professional expertise. And if you feel the need for some extra support, please talk to your GP who can help to point you in the right direction, or contact the British Association for Behavioural and Cognitive Psychotherapies (www.babcp.com) who have a register of accredited therapists. Please don't struggle with this alone. And remember that there are various other therapeutic approaches available; these are just the ones that I have found helpful.

Cognitive Behavioural Therapy (CBT)

CBT can help you change the way you think (cognitive) and what you do (behaviour), and these changes can help to make you feel better. It's a way of talking about how you view and think about yourself, the world and other people, and how what you do affects the way you think and feel. Over our lifetimes, and especially after significant losses or traumas, our self-perception can become very fixed, and not always in a good way. This in turn can affect the way we behave, or view the world, or relate to other people.

In CBT a therapist will help you to break down a problem which seems overwhelming into five different aspects: the situation, your thoughts about it, your emotions, your physical feelings and your actions in response to it. All of these are interconnected, and what happens in one area can affect all of the others. How you think about a problem can affect the way you feel about it, physically and emotionally. There are different ways of reacting to any situation – and this can be either helpful, or not. CBT can help you learn to react to situations in a more helpful (or positive) way. This can be particularly true after a bereavement because being distressed can lead us to misread situations, jump to conclusions or react to situations in unhelpful ways. Our usual benchmarks or 'good sense compasses' are malfunctioning. CBT can support you to regain a sense of perspective in this regard, and to 're-think' your connection with the world.

You can do CBT one to one with a therapist, in a group, or using a book to guide you independently. I found a one-to-one situation most helpful: I knew I needed to share some difficult thoughts and feelings, and didn't feel able to do that in a group setting. But I also knew I didn't have the discipline to follow through with a self-guided CBT course.

Although CBT is concerned with 'the here and now' and looking ahead, a therapist will talk with you about issues from your past life and background, to see how this might be affecting you now. They are also likely to ask you to keep a diary to record how you think and feel in response to different situations. This helps to identify your patterns of thinking and behaving, and whether these might be unhelpful or unrealistic. The therapist will then suggest ways of changing these patterns of thinking and behaving, and you can make plans together for 'homework' to practise the new ways of doing both. At subsequent sessions you will discuss how easy, or not, you find this. Throughout, you will be able to dictate the level at which you do any of this; the pace of working through this will be guided by you.

CBT has been found to be very effective in helping people with anxiety or depression; as effective, in fact, as anti-depressants for many forms of depression. And because it helps you to find new ways of thinking and behaving, these are strategies that last, and which you can continue practising throughout your life. (And they do need to be practised; I am only too aware of falling back into lazy, negative ways of thinking, which are definitely not helpful if I don't keep remembering my CBT lessons.)

It doesn't offer a quick fix, though; and it may be that if you are feeling very low, it's too hard to manage at that point. When I was at my lowest ebb, as I said earlier, I was prescribed anti-anxiety medication at the time when I did CBT. I'm sure this helped me regain enough connection with my real self to then be open to the work I needed to complete with my CBT therapist. Even then, there were some sessions when I fought the process. It can be quite confrontational – the sources of anxiety or depression can be deep seated, and confronting them honestly can be challenging and distressing. At one stage I decided I'd had enough of doing that, and told the therapist I wouldn't be continuing. But he helped me look at my reasons for that, and we picked my defensiveness apart – and I'm so glad we did, because the best work followed from that.

A course of CBT can last between six weeks and six months. You might need to have a 'refresher' course subsequently. There is no evidence of CBT doing any harm, but it might not feel right for you at a given time, and another therapeutic approach might feel more effective. However, for many people, it has significant, meaningful and life-enhancing benefits.

Mindfulness

Mindfulness involves paying really close attention to 'being in the moment', in terms of what you are thinking, feeling or doing. It has its roots in Buddhist principles, and as such, can be related to certain types of meditation. But it isn't religious (although can be used in religious contexts) and you don't have to sit cross legged chanting a mantra. Once you have learned the basic techniques, mindfulness can be practised anywhere, doing anything. It can be very helpful in improving people's mental health or sense of wellbeing, and research has shown that it can help people to manage certain kinds of anxiety and mild depression.

You can learn mindfulness in a group led by trained practitioners, from online courses, or self-guided, from a book. Accredited course leaders can be found online or through your GP.

A bit like CBT, mindfulness has at its core the idea that ingrained patterns of thought are not always helpful, and may not accurately reflect reality. For example, I've related the feelings of anxiety I had about going to big gatherings of friends after Jon died. A lot of these feelings were based on my thoughts and beliefs that I would definitely have a bad time, because I'd be sad, or feel like the odd one out, or generally just hate every minute. Some of these thoughts were based on past experience – but in reality, the party was never as bad as I feared, and if I could get beyond the negative, unhelpful thoughts, I even managed to have a good time. Mindfulness helps you to practise gently pushing the unhelpful (or stressful) thoughts away, and connect with your underlying feelings so that you can approach life with a more objective, optimistic or accepting mind. It helps you to control your feelings by understanding and recognising your thought patterns.

To do this, you practise focusing on the here and now. When you start out, it's easiest to practise this sitting quietly, thinking in detail about (being mindful of) your breathing, how your body feels, and how your thoughts are coming and going. I joined a mindfulness group (as with the CBT, I knew I wouldn't be disciplined enough to set time aside to practise by myself). The first exercise we did was mindfully eating a giant sultana. Don't knock it until you've tried it. We were encouraged to hold the sultana in our hand and think about how it felt: smell it, touch it, look at it. Then we put it in our mouths, concentrating on how it tasted, how it felt in our mouths – what the whole process of eating it felt like. And we were meant to gently push away any non-sultana based thoughts while we were doing it.

Once we'd got past the slightly embarrassing experience of sitting in a circle of strangers, eyes shut, slowly chewing pieces of dried fruit, we began to understand what being mindful was about – really being in the moment, focusing only on the one thing that was most important at that time. Not thinking about what had gone before, or what was going to come later.

During the course, we were encouraged to always be compassionate to ourselves, and to observe our thought patterns without criticism. Rather than reacting emotionally, or with frustration, to thoughts that intruded on our mindfulness practice, we learned to just let them go, and bring our focus back onto our breathing, or our connection with the feelings in different parts of our body. It was important not to take negative or unhelpful thoughts personally, but to learn to let them drift out of our consciousness. The point of all this practice was to learn to catch the darker thoughts before they spiralled downwards, and to regain control of our feelings.

If you're reading this and thinking 'nope…all far too touchy-feely, self-revealing, scary stuff for me', please be reassured that I felt exactly the same at the outset. But by the end of the course we were all completely comfortable lying on the floor together, in our own mindful space; and we voluntarily signed up for a full day of lying around on the floor (and other equally helpful exercises) before the 10 weeks were up.

With practice, you can stand back from your thoughts, see them objectively and train yourself to recognise when they're taking over. You can control them, and not vice versa. And you don't have to sit quietly for long periods of time to be mindful. You can do anything mindfully – try washing the dishes, only focusing on the task in hand, thinking about each thing you clean, how your body is feeling while you do it, gently pushing away any non-dish based thoughts while you do it. It can give your busy, tired brain a real break.

There's a lot more to mindfulness, but for me, this was the crux – giving my head a break, and stopping the stressful thoughts overloading me.

You can read online about different types of mindfulness course, and which ones might work for you. It isn't right for everyone, and especially not if you're feeling particularly low: it does require connecting with potentially challenging or difficult thoughts. You may also not feel comfortable in a group setting, and you may not have the time or energy to practise the techniques just now. There may be a different, more appropriate source of support if this is the case. As with CBT, it is advisable to discuss starting a mindfulness course, or alternatives, with your GP.

ADVICE AND INFORMATION SHEETS
FROM WINSTON'S WISH

These are some of the activities and ideas which we found helpful at different times after Jon's death. Please note there are more up-to-date handouts available from Winston's Wish, which families who contact them may receive instead of these.

---

10 WAYS TO REMEMBER PEOPLE ON SPECIAL DAYS, MAYBE THEIR BIRTHDAY OR THE ANNIVERSARY OF THEIR DEATH

- Take a special card to their grave – or to where their ashes were buried or scattered.
- Tie a card or a special message to a helium balloon and let it soar into the sky.
- Blow some bubbles and send them your love on the wind.
- Plant some bulbs or a shrub in a place that holds special memories of the person who has died – what was their favourite colour?
- Have their favourite meal – Fish and chips? Roast dinner? Curry?
- Listen to their favourite music.
- Begin to make a memory box in which to keep things that remind you of the person – photos, shells, holiday snaps, glasses, earrings.
- Ask other people for their memories of the person who dies and begin to compile their 'life story'.
- Write them a letter or a poem or a song. Maybe you could start with something like 'if you came back for just five minutes, I'd tell you…'

the charity for bereaved children

A CALENDAR OF MEMORIES

Remembering Important Dates

When someone in a child's family has died there are often many dates in the year that are important.

Some dates are more obvious than others, for example, Christmas Day, Chinese New Year, Ramadan or celebrating Father's or Mother's Day. Only the child may know particular dates that are important, such as the date that would have been the person's birthday, the date they died, or the start of the football season (because their relative liked football).

It is impossible for someone outside the family to remember all these dates; however, it may be helpful to find a way of doing this so the child can feel supported and valued at these times.

Making a list of dates

- Try to make time to meet with the child a few weeks after the person has died.
- Explain why you want to make a list of dates – brainstorm a list of dates.
- The list could include important cultural or religious dates, days that are special in their family such as birthdays, the day the person died or the date of the funeral.
- The list could also include other dates that are important to the family: *'On the first day of the summer holidays we always went out for breakfast'* or *'We always had an Easter egg hunt on Easter Day.'*
- Discuss with the child the fact that you will also keep a copy of the calendar – so you can think of them on these days.

What about Father's and Mother's Day?

Many people worry that making a card to celebrate Father's or Mother's Day may be upsetting for a child whose father or mother has died.

It is often best to ask a child what they want to do, simply by saying 'I know your daddy has died, other children make Father's Day cards – what would you like to do this year?'

It is important to give a child options. If they decide to make a card, talk with them about where to put it. They may want to take it to the grave, keep it by a picture of the person who dies or put it safely in their memory box where they collect other special mementoes.

Try to help the child think of...

Things they can do on difficult days

- Talk about the person who has died.
- Write a letter to them.
- Eat their favourite meal.
- Watch a video of them.
- Wear their jumper.
- Light a candle.
- Visit the grave.
- Look at photos.
- Listen to some music.
- Cry, laugh.
- Let a balloon go with a message.
- Do nothing – take some time out just to think.

Winston's Wish
the charity for bereaved children

MAKING A JAR OF MEMORIES

You may like to make a coloured 'Salt Sculpture' to help you remember important things about the person who has died.

You will need
- A small jar with a lid and wide neck (e.g. baby food jar)
- Salt
- 5 coloured chalks
- 6 pieces of paper

What to do
1. Fill your jar to the brim with salt. On one of the pieces of paper write down 5 things you remember about the person who has died. These could be things you know they liked, something they enjoyed doing, perhaps somewhere you went together or what you remember about them as a person. Then choose a different colour to represent each memory and put a dot of that colour next to each memory.
2. Spread out 5 sheets of paper and divide the salt from the jar between them.
3. Then colour each pile of salt using one of the 5 chalks. Rub each chalk backwards and forwards into the salt. The salt will begin to take on the colour of the chalk. The harder you rub the brighter the coloured salt will become.
4. Carefully pick up each piece of paper and pour the coloured salts into your jar one at a time. (If you tilt your jar you can make waves of colour appear.)

5. When all the colours have been added, hold the jar and tap it down on a work surface to settle the salt. Do not shake the jar unless you want to mix up all the colours. Then fill any remaining space with plain salt (right up to the very top!). This is important and will prevent the colours mixing.

6. Secure the lid firmly and use some sellotape to hold it in place. Try to keep your list of what the colours mean to you close by the jar. You may like to show other people in your family your 'jar of memories'. Can you thing of a special place where you can put your jar?

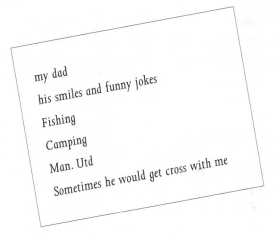

my dad
his smiles and funny jokes
Fishing
Camping
Man. Utd
Sometimes he would get cross with me

the charity for bereaved children

157

THE CHARTER FOR BEREAVED CHILDREN

Winston's Wish is the leading childhood bereavement charity and the largest provider of services to bereaved families. This 'charter' is based on our conversations with thousands of children and their families. They have told us what helps them to rebuild their lives and face the future with hope.

B Bereavement support

Bereaved children need to receive support from their family, from their school and from important people around them.

'It's OK to cry and it's OK to be happy as well.'
James (12)

E Express feelings and thoughts

Bereaved children should be helped to find appropriate ways to express all their feelings and thoughts associated with grief, such as sadness, anxiety, confusion, anger and guilt.

'Mum died of a heart attack but I don't understand why it attacked her.'
Bethany (4)

R Remember the person who has died

Bereaved children have the right to remember the person who has died for the rest of their lives, sharing special as well as difficult memories.

'I helped dad choose the flowers for mum's funeral. I felt proud of that.'
Tim (7)

'It was good to be with other people who had an idea of what I was going through.'
Chris (13)

E Education and information

Bereaved children need and are entitled to receive answers to their questions and information that clearly explains what has happened, why it has happened and what will be happening.

A Appropriate response from schools and colleges

Bereaved children need understanding and support from their teachers and fellow students without having to ask for it.

V Voice in important decisions

Bereaved children should be given the choice about their involvement in important decisions that have an impact on their lives such as planning the funeral and remembering anniversaries.

E Enjoyment

Bereaved children have the right to enjoy their lives even though someone important has died.

M Meet others

Bereaved children benefit from the opportunity to meet other children who have had similar experiences.

E Established routines

Bereaved children should, whenever possible, be able to continue activities and interests so tht parts of their lives can still feel 'normal'.

'I now understand that it wasn't something I did or didn't do that made her die.'
Neela (16)

'It helped to know that other people understood what I was going through.'
Rachel (9)

'I like to show my memory box to people who didn't know my dad.'
Paul (15)

'My teacher remembers that days that are difficult like Father's Day and his birthday.'
Alex (10)

'Seeing my son meeting other children in the same situation as him was so helpful.'
John (parent)

N Not to blame

Bereaved children should be helped to understand that they are not responsible, and not to blame, for the death.

'I kept going to swimming club. I thought about my brother while I swam.'
Amy (14)

T Tell the story

Bereaved children are helped by being encouraged to tell an accurate and coherent story of what has happened. These stories need to be heard by those important people in their lives.

'My picture shows how the car missed me but knocked dad off his bike.'
Sophie (9)

the charity for bereaved children